Property and Casualty Insurance Concepts Simplified

Property and Casualty Insurance Concepts Simplified

The Ultimate 'How To' Insurance Guide for Agents, Brokers, Underwriters and Adjusters

Christopher J. Boggs

CPCU, ARM, ALCM, LPCS, AAI, APA, CWCA, CRIS, AINS

Contents

Chapter 1

How to Read an Insurance Policy

When did you last read the entire commercial general liability policy, commercial property policy or any insurance policy from beginning to end just as a refresher? Rarely does any insurance practitioner. Generally there is a specific answer being sought or problem being researched requiring review of only individual parts of the form and its applicable endorsements to develop an answer or opinion.

Insurance professionals realize that answering a coverage question or providing an opinion without first reviewing the policy (and applicable endorsements) is errors and omissions quicksand. But once the complete policy is in-hand, certain "rules" can be applied in reading the form to make finding the needed answer easier and quicker. These are not shortcuts to reading the policy, just pointers to make finding the most correct answer easier.

Twelve Rules for Reading an Insurance Policy

1. Ascertain who qualifies as an insured. If the person or entity suffering or causing the loss, injury or damage is not an insured, there is no need to go any further – there is no coverage. Remember, there are four levels of insureds: 1) named insured(s) (first and all listed), 2)

1

extended insureds, 3) automatic insureds, and 4) additional (endorsed) insureds.

2. Annotate the policy form by highlighting the areas changed by an endorsement and list which endorsement changes that section. When reading that part, apply the endorsement wording directly.

3. Compare the forms and endorsements listed on the declarations page with the forms and endorsements attached to make sure the entire policy is available. This includes confirming the edition dates match.

4. Read the ***Insuring Agreement*** first to make sure the loss or occurrence is contemplated. This is the broadest the coverage is ever going to be – so start here.

5. After the insuring agreement, read the exclusions. In most liability and special form property policies, coverage is created when not excluded. Treat named peril property policies and the "personal and advertising injury" section of the commercial general liability policy differently, read the list of covered perils (that which causes a loss) first, then the exclusions.

6. Read the exceptions to the exclusions. Exceptions give coverage back in specific amounts. As is discussed in Chapter 2, "Six Reasons the Loss is Excluded," it's easier for the carrier to give coverage back by exception than to delete coverage using a long list of exclusions.

7. When the policy refers to another section, read that section immediately.

8. Pay attention to the conjunctions used in a list. "And" is inclusive, "or" is exclusive. If there is a list of five qualifiers, the use of "and" means that all five must be satisfied. "Or" means that if any of the five apply, coverage is granted or excluded (or whatever the list provides).

9. Pay attention to key words and phrases. There are certain key words that must be underlined or highlighted when reading the policy. These words and phrases create, delete or alter coverage and limits (this may not be an all-inclusive list):

    - "Not" as in "does not apply to..." or "does not include..." This changes or limits whatever grant or denial of coverage preceded it.

    - "Greater than...," "lesser than...," "Greater of...," "lesser of...," "no more than...," "the most...," "all..." or any other quantifying phrase. "The insured receives the 'lesser of'..." is a quantifying phrase indicating that of the upcoming values, the insured will get the least or lowest amount.

    - "Unless...," "except...," "only if..." or "subject to..." each connotes a change in condition, added requirement or an alternative.

    - "However" discounts everything before it. This is a qualifying term that creates coverage or condition parameters.

- "Includes," as the name suggests, is an inclusive term that broadens the provision to which it applies.
- "Must" and "regardless" There is no alternative and surrounding circumstances are of no consideration in meeting the requirement.
- "First" is an order of sequence term. Some policy provisions list the order of events or actions. Particular attention must be given to the order of events prescribed by these sequencing terms.

10. Read and understand the definitions of specifically defined terms. The insurance carrier desires to control the meaning of certain words and phrases and does so by specifically defining them in the policy. Such definitions can limit or explain the breadth of protection. Words not defined are given their common, everyday meaning.
11. Understand and make sure all the policy conditions have been met. Failure to meet the policy's conditions can result in the denial of coverage.
12. Confirm the coverage limits are adequate for the loss. Pay attention to the conjunctions used in a list.

Does Coverage Exist

Applying these policy-review rules will allow quicker coverage determinations, subject, of course, to the specific situation and surrounding laws. Exhibit 1.1 is a loss/claims worksheet to guide the user through the policy to determine the availability of coverage.

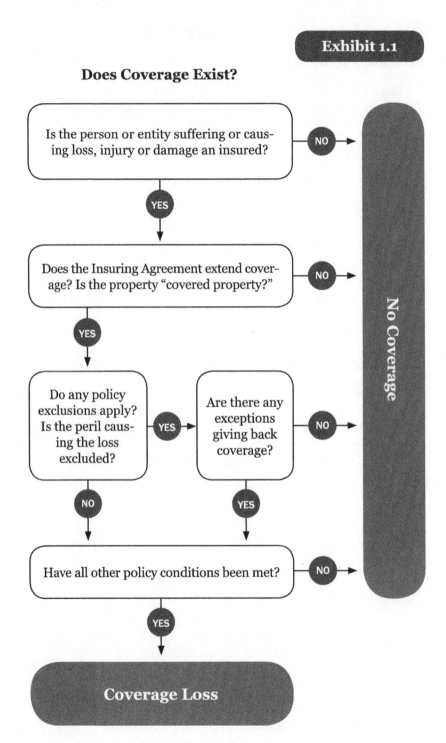

Exhibit 1.1

Does Coverage Exist?

Chapter 2

Six Reasons the Loss is Excluded

Insurance was created as a mechanism to protect insureds against the financial consequences of an unforeseen, potentially catastrophic individual loss. The number of covered perils has expanded and contracted over time to match the changes in exposure's severity, frequency and ultimate costs, but the original concept of protecting the insured's financial condition as not changed. However, insureds are not protected against every possible source of financial loss.

Traditional insurance policies contain a list or description of incidents, causes or results not covered. This is true whether reading a property or liability form and regardless whether the insured is a commercial or personal lines client. Exclusions always exist and there is a reason for each one.

Exclusion Categories

To understand the six reasons for each exclusion first requires knowledge of the three broad categories of exclusions. The three categories of exclusions are: 1) excluded "perils," 2) excluded "hazards," and 3) excluded "property." A "peril" is the actual cause of the damage resulting in financial loss (i.e. fire). A "hazard" is anything that increase the likelihood that a

7

financial loss or "peril" will occur (i.e. frayed wires (the hazard) may cause a fire (the peril)).

Excluded perils and excluded hazards are not equal in their ultimate effect on the insured. "***Excluded perils***" can generally (but not always) be remedied either by an exception to the exclusion, an endorsement or the purchase of a separate policy. Conversely, "***excluded hazards***" are almost always absolute with little possibility of plugging the hole created by the exclusion or broadening any coverage that may be given by an exception to the exclusion.

For example an insured can purchase earthquake coverage, but even difference in condition (DIC) forms exclude war, leaving the insured no reasonable recourse. Earth movement is the peril, the cause of the loss, whereas war or military action simply increases the chance that something is going to happen. The war itself doesn't cause a loss; it's just a hazard that increases the chance of a loss.

Some exclusions walk the line between "excluded peril" and "excluded hazard." The "***Ordinance or Law***" exclusion is an example. Ordinance or law is a "peril" because the enforcement of building codes actually does cause a financial loss, but it's also a hazard because the condition of being "out of code" increases the amount of the loss and the possibility that a peril will occur.

"***Excluded property***" is somewhat self-explanatory. Under the commercial property form there is no coverage for the property of others in the insured's care, custody or control (with some exceptions). Both are "property"- related exclusions.

Why is it Excluded?

From the three broad exclusionary categories flow the six reasons for exclusions. Nearly all policy exclusions arise from one of the following.

1. The peril, or property is better covered elsewhere.
2. The loss or damage is collectively catastrophic in nature.
3. The loss or damage is not accidental or unforeseen.
4. The insurance carrier is willing to provide coverage, they just want more information and more premium.
5. The insurance carrier wants to control the amount of coverage granted.
6. The loss results from a "speculative" or business risk.

The Peril, Hazard or Property can be Better Covered

Some exclusions exist because there is a more appropriate coverage form available to provide the needed protection. Money loss is excluded in the commercial property form because this exposure is better covered under a **crime policy**. Likewise, the use of an auto is excluded under the commercial general liability policy because the **auto policy** is the more appropriate place for coverage.

Property and liability forms both contain exclusions existing simply because the particular form was not created for that specific exposure. It is incumbent upon the agent to cover those exposures with the appropriate policy.

The final reason for the use of separate policies is the threat of <u>adverse selection</u> (see definition). Some perils and hazards are such that only those in danger of suffering such loss are willing to pay for the coverage. If only a small number of insureds buys the coverage, the insurer would not have the necessary funds to pay the potential losses, which would require higher premiums – resulting in fewer insureds (thus begins the adverse selection spiral). Some of these excluded losses also fall under the catastrophic loss exclusion.

The Loss or Damage is Collectively Catastrophic in Nature

Insurance was not designed to respond to community disasters, only to individual "disasters." Certain perils and hazards have the potential to result in wide-spread damage the industry is not structured to handle, nor is the consuming public willing to pay the additional premium to finance coverage for catastrophic losses in their policies.

Two "adverse selection" exclusions, as discussed in the previous section, within the commercial property form also fall under the "catastrophic" loss category. Flood and earthquake damage can be insured by purchasing other coverage, but damage by these perils is considered catastrophic so coverage is not provided in most standard property forms.

The Loss or Damage is not Accidental or Unforeseen by the Insured

An "insurable loss" is one that is accidental, unforeseen, definite in time and place and is measurable. Intentional acts of the insured or intended results are excluded in nearly every insurance policy, property or liability. Also falling outside the definition of "insurable loss" are losses that are likely to (or will) happen, damage specifically controllable by the insured and known events.

- *Exclusions for losses that are likely (or will) happen:* Wear and tear to property is going to happen, as does general deterioration. The insurance company is not going to insure something guaranteed to happen (the policy would then be a warranty rather than insurance).

- *The insured can control the loss:* This eliminates coverage for intentional acts, damage over long periods of time and failure to care for the property (not maintaining heat to keep water pipes from freezing). An example in the CGL is the violation of SPAM laws.

- *Exclusion for known or previously occurring events:* This eliminates coverage for losses that the insured knew about prior to the policy period or began prior to coverage being enacted.

Insurance Carrier Wants More Information and Premium

Endorsements are available to remove or narrow the breadth of some policy exclusions, allowing the insured to customize coverage to fit its needs. Insurance policies are, to some extent, written with the "average" insured in mind. Not doing this would increase premiums for all insureds – even when some have no need for the additional coverage. Other-than-average insureds with special exposures or needs have the option to endorse away various exclusions.

Additionally, before granting extended coverage insurance carriers often want more information about the insured plus some additional premium. This allows some level of policy customization for unique insureds while maintaining an appropriate premium for the risk but without discriminating unfairly against insureds which do not need the same breadth of coverage.

Insurance Carrier Wants to Control the Amount of Coverage Granted

As an example, the commercial property policy specifically excludes loss caused by collapse, but then it gives back some coverage for loss caused by collapse under the "Additional Coverage" section. Excluding coverage only to give it back under another section (or even in the same section) seems to perpetuate the public's perception that insurance is confusing. But this method is not as counterintuitive as it first appears.

Excluding coverage and giving some of it back allows the insurance carrier to dictate the exact amount of coverage they are willing to offer. They control the breadth of coverage. Compare that with trying to give the coverage outright then limit it with exclusions. There is no way that all possible situations could be imagined leading to confusion and likely court involvement.

Taking coverage away and giving it back in pre-determined amounts makes far more sense and reduces the potential for confusion. This tactic is used in property and liability coverage forms.

Speculative or Business Risk Exclusions

"Pure risk" has only two possibilities, something bad happens or nothing happens. There is no possibility for gain. The insured enjoys a "zero sum year" or suffers a financial loss. Pure risk, also known as absolute risk, is insurable. Its counterpart is "speculative risk."

"Speculative risk" (or "business risk") involves the chances of loss, of no change or gain. Insurance is not designed to protect the insured from a bad investment or bad business decision.

Examples of speculative risk exclusions include the CGL's product recall exclusion (which can be covered by endorsements) and the commercial property policy's special causes of loss exclusions "voluntary parting" and "delay, loss of use or loss of market."

Conditional Conclusion

The insurance contract is a conditional contract. Excluded perils, excluded hazards and excluded property are part of the conditions. When viewed in the light of reason, policy exclusions are not unreasonable – even if the insured thinks they are.

Without many of the exclusions contained in property and liability policies, premiums would be prohibitively high and fewer viable carriers would be available to accept the risk.

Compare this list of six reasons to any property or liability policy when explaining coverage and exclusions to the insured. The list can also be used to uncover the insured's exposures that require other coverage forms or customizing endorsements.

Chapter 3

Insurance Premiums are Only a Small Part of the Insured's Total Cost of Risk

So many insureds complain about the price of their insurance. Rarely does a client say, *"That premium seems fair; the insurance company is getting adequate premium to cover its exposure and I'm getting the protection I need."* No, the most often heard complaint is, *"I can't believe I have to pay out all this money. The insurance company is killing me. Can't we get the premium down?"*

Carriers such as GEICO, Progressive and now Allstate are playing to the belief that insurance is all about the premium/price. But is it the price or the cost the insured needs to calculate? Insureds must understand or be taught that the premium (price) is only part of their **"Total Cost of Risk."**

Every insured is subject, in varying degrees, to the "total cost of risk" concept, from the personal lines client up to the largest Fortune 500 Corporation. Six "costs" in addition to the premium combine to develop the insured's true cost of risk: 1) Deductibles/Self-Insured Retentions, 2) The cost of uninsured and/or self-insured losses, 3) Legal costs, 4) Loss control and safety costs, 5) Claims management, and 6) Opportunity costs.

Deductibles and Self-Insured Retentions

Premium savings is often accomplished by increasing the deductible or self-insured retention. But any price savings must be weighed against the "out-of-pocket" cost directly related to the deductible. The Price/Cost comparison is easy with smaller clients that have relatively few losses. A small commercial client, for example, may enjoy a premium savings of $2,000 by going from a $1,000 property deductible to a $5,000 property deductible, but one loss could "cost" the insured $3,000 more than staying with the lower deductible.

The Price-Cost comparison is complicated when the premium difference is in the multiple-thousands of dollars range. Successfully calculating the true cost savings requires an analysis of the loss history and the development of loss projections. While there is no guarantee that what happened in the past (as all loss (past and future) are random events), will occur in the future it's the only way to develop some comparison.

Larger corporations are major proponents of high deductible programs because there is the immediate premium savings (as seen on the balance sheet). But when compared to the actual cost of loss experience such plan may be more expensive (but the cost may be spread over multiple accounting periods).

Basically, premium savings are eaten away by the cost of deductibles and self-insured retentions.

Uninsured and Self-Insured Losses

In an effort to cut the insurance price, insureds may intentionally or worse, unintentionally, self-insure certain risks. Intentional self-insurance requires careful study of loss frequency and more importantly loss severity before implementation. Unintentional self-insurance is what happens when price is the main concern and coverages are chopped to lower the premium.

Any out-of-pocket expense related to self-insurance is part of the insured's total cost of risk. Like the use of deductible/self-insured retentions, these may push the cost of risk beyond the pre-change price of insurance.

Legal Costs

Defending uninsured or self-insured events or losses can be expensive. The cost of defense counsel can devour any premium savings previously enjoyed. Legal cost as part of the total cost of risk is, on one side, a function of the two previous decisions.

On its other side are the legal costs incurred to avoid a financial loss. This includes the cost to develop proper contractual risk transfer mechanisms and employee manuals (just two examples).

Loss Control and Safety Costs

In an effort to avoid or reduce loss, some insureds may invest in loss control and safety. This includes safety devices such as sprinkler systems and safety equipment like safety glasses and fall protection. Granted, some of these are required by regulation, but such costs arise out of the inherent risk of the operation and are thus part of the "total cost of risk."

Claims Management

Losses subject to a self-insured retention, self-insured losses and uninsured losses must be managed by someone. This someone may be an internal employee designated as the claims administrator or it may be an outside administrator – often known as a third party administrator (TPA).

Although the expense of the internal employee may be captured under a separate line item – payroll expense – the cost is still a part of the total cost of risk. TPA expense is also a part of the cost.

Without either of these individuals available, the cost of a single loss could escalate beyond what it should be (especially in workers' compensation), catapulting the total cost of risk far above the price of traditional insurance.

Someone has to manage claims, and the costs associated make up part of the total cost of risk.

Opportunity Cost

A somewhat subjective cost is the opportunity cost. In order to manage a non-traditional (or even traditional) insurance program requires that resources be taken from other areas of the operation. These are monetary and time resources.

The insured can choose to pay a higher premium to allow the insurance company to pay their personnel to do the work, or they can choose to do some parts of it themselves. This comes back to a price-cost analysis.

Payroll and time costs are a factor in the total cost of the insured's risk.

Price vs. Cost

Insureds can ALWAYS find a lower price – but at what COST? Understanding the Total Cost of Risk concept is important to both insureds and agents. Being able to distinguish between the two can save insureds in the long run.

Don't misunderstand, there is a place for alternative programs and even some price comparison among the less sophisticated coverages, but don't ever let the insured, or yourself, be fooled into thinking that insurance is all about price.

Chapter 4

Is Your Client a Risk Taker?

Agents just assume that a particular client is risk averse because they have never asked about alternative risk financing techniques. It's possible the insured is not aware of the existence of such plans. Adequately serving these clients necessitates exploring all the alternatives available to finance their risk of loss.

As was discussed in Chapter 3, "Insurance Premiums are Only a Small Part of the Insured's Total Cost of Risk," insureds already have a cost of risk that exceeds the insurance premium. The larger the insured, the higher the cost of risk in excess of paid insurance premiums. Might that medium-to-large insured be willing to accept a potential expensive downside in exchange for an equally beneficial upside savings in the total cost of risk? One way to find out is to ask.

Exhibit 4.1 is a tool agents can use to explore the insured's attitude toward risk. This survey asks 18 pointed questions regarding the insured's financial condition, internal controls, loss history, loss predictability and desire and ability to be actively involved in claims.

Each question is ranked on a 1 to 5 scale. The higher the number the more the insured AGREES with the statement presented. Thus, "1" indicates strong disagreement and "5" translates into strong agreement. The higher the score, the more willing the insured is to explore alternative risk financing techniques. Each level can point to different programs.

- **Low** (18-30) – Traditional Insurance (First Dollar). Not ready for too much unexpected.
- **Low-to-Medium** (31-45) – Might want to consider a retrospective type plan for liability coupled with a high deductible property program.
- **Medium** (46-60) – A high deductible program for casualty lines along with the same for property lines. Casualty lines would require a stop-loss provision of some type.
- **Medium-to-High** (61-75) – A high deductible program for all lines with no aggregate or stop loss. Essentially the amount out of pocket is unlimited with the exception of the per-occurrence deductible. A protected cell captive may also be an option.
- **High** (76-90) – Insureds in this range may be ready for a captive without a stop loss or a fully self-insured program.

The considerations based on the score are just possibilities and not hard-and-fast rules. Whether a particular program is right for an insured, regardless of their score, is subject to the design of the program and the current condition of the insured. Conditions and needs change and what may be "right" for the insured now may not be the correct plan three or four years from now.

Don't limit this survey to just the CEO, president or owner. Have all the top managers complete the survey. Each has a different perspective and a better understanding of their area of responsibility than the others. Total the scores from each participant and take the average (giving no one opinion greater weight than another) – that will be the level of risk acceptance or aversion of the entity as a whole.

"Risk Taker" Questionnaire

Exhibit 4.1

Statement	Rating (1-5)*
We are willing to risk potentially very high "out-of-pocket" costs for property and liability losses in exchange for potentially great savings in our risk financing program.	
Large fluctuations in our cost of risk are easily absorbed into our operating cost.	
We have a favorable credit rating that will not be seriously affected by the need to provide a Letter of Credit (LOC). Future credit needs are not in jeopardy because of an LOC.	
Large unexpected loss-related expenses can be easily covered from available capital.	
We have an active loss control program in place to protect plant, people and contents from injury or damage.	
Our safety and loss control program and procedures are stringently enforced on and at all levels of personnel.	
Upper management actively promotes, participates in and models the loss control and risk management program and procedures in place.	
We are willing to make all necessary investments in safety (including but is not limited to safety equipment, machine guards and full-time or consulting loss control personnel).	
We make full use of contractual risk transfer and any available insurance transfer (requesting addition as an additional insured, etc.) anytime we contract work to an external entity.	
All safety and security systems are well maintained and regularly inspected to insure proper response when needed.	
Every employee is well-trained in the job they do (and cross-trained where necessary). Also, the employee is versed in all loss control and risk management procedures.	
Our claims (property and casualty) are relatively predictable within a narrow margin from year to year.	
We want to take an active role in managing our claims and losses.	
We have the staff necessary to internally manage our claims and losses.	
We are willing to hire the staff necessary to manage our claims and losses.	
We are willing to learn and comply with all statutory requirements necessary to manage our own claims and losses.	
We have access to and a relationship with counsel well-versed in insurance law and property and casualty insurance claims management.	
We are willing and able to set funds aside for claims and losses without the need to use those funds later for other purposes.	

*1= Strongly Disagree; 3= Neutral; 5= Strongly Agree

Chapter 5

Understanding the Basics of Contractual Risk Transfer

Vicarious liability is created when one person or entity is or can be held legally liable for the results of another person's or entity's actions. Such indirect liability can arise out of a relationship (parent/child, employer/employee, etc.), position or contract. Also required is the right, ability or duty to control the actions of the directly liable party. Without the opportunity or responsibility to control another's actions there can be no vicarious liability.

Owners, general contractors and others can hold positions with a certain amount of control over and responsibility for the actions of lower tier contractors or independent contractors. This control leaves them vulnerable to being held vicariously liable for the actions of these lower-level entities in addition to any liability for their own actions.

Contractual risk transfer is a mechanism for managing such indirect liability and is wholly separate from any contractual requirement to purchase or provide insurance protection. When (and to the extent allowable,) contractual risk transfer is used to avoid, or attempt to avoid, the financial consequences of being held liable for the actions or inactions of another (and sometimes for one's own actions).

This chapter: 1) defines contractual risk transfer, 2) lists the three parties involved in risk transfer, 3) describes the three levels of transfer, and 4) discusses the basics of contractual risk transfer wording.

Contractual Risk Transfer

Contractual Risk Transfer is a non-insurance contract/agreement between two parties whereby one agrees to indemnify and hold another party harmless for specified actions, inactions, injuries or damages. Risk transfer accomplishes objectives found in both risk financing (finding a source to pay the cost of a claim) and risk control (developing a means to avoid or lessen the cost of loss).

The ideal use and true purpose of contractual risk transfer is to place the financial burden of a loss on the party best able to control or prevent the incident leading to injury or damage. Presumably, the entity(ies) directly and actively participating in the activity have the best opportunity to prevent or avoid the loss. Thus, they are contractually required to protect an "innocent" supervising or non-participating party from financial harm following injury or damage.

However, some "transferors" (defined below) violate contractual risk transfer's use and purpose by contractually attempting to **absolve** themselves of responsibility for, or avoid the financial consequences of, generally non-transferable liability for injury or damage. Such broad risk transfer, sometimes called as **exculpatory agreements**, requires the "transferee" (see below) to stand in the place of the transferor regardless of who caused the loss, even if the transferor was solely responsible for the injury or damage. Such broad wording may not be enforceable, depending on jurisdiction's law (10 states allow such wording in construction contracts under specific circumstances) and the totality of the circumstances under which the contract was drawn and presented.

Contracts, as a rule, cannot be used to transfer or avoid statutory requirements, common law duties, criminal penalties or sole negligence in tort. Wording that violates these rules of contract construction may be considered exculpatory. Whether a contract 1) contains exculpatory provisions, and 2) is ultimately enforceable is judged against four criteria.

- ***The existence of a duty to the public***. The greater the duty owed to the public, the less likely the entity involved in the operation can transfer the legal liability to another party ("transferee"). For example, entities subject to strict (or absolute) liability, such as blasting contractors, cannot transfer their liability.

- ***The nature of the service performed***. The higher the intrinsic hazard, the less likely liability for the results of the activity can be contractually transferred.

- ***Whether the contract was entered into fairly.*** Was the contract on a "take-it-or-leave-it" basis or was there room for negotiation? Was the contract unilaterally beneficial or bilaterally beneficial (did both parties gain something of value)? Was there time to review the contract? Was the contract signed before the work began? Did one party have an unfair advantage in the contracting process? These and other specific questions relate to the fairness of the contract.

- ***Whether the intentions of the parties are expressed in clear, unambiguous language.*** Contracts considered ambiguous are generally interpreted in favor of the party that did not participate in, or had very little participation in, the development of the contract.

Historically courts avoid negating contracts and individual contract provisions (although that may change in the coming years) because the right to enter into a contract is considered a personal right and responsibility generally valued by the courts. But nearly any court that adjudicates a contract 1) which violates statues, 2) is considered unconscionable, or 3) is against public policy will likely strictly construe the contract against the party who produced it – if not voiding the contract or contractual transfer provision outright.

Contractual Risk Transfer and the "Rules of Threes"

There are three parties to (and three levels of) contractual risk transfer, thus the "rule of threes." Although not an actual rule, this is an easy way to remember these two important concepts surrounding contractual risk transfer.

There are three parties having a part in contractual risk transfer.

- **Transferors** – The party transferring its risk of financial loss to another. This may include the owner, the project management firm, and/or the general contractor. Other common terms for the transferor include "***indemnitee***" and "***promisee***."

- **Transferees** – The party accepting the risk. This can include the general contractor and subcontractors. "***indemnitor***" and "***promisor***" are other names for a transferee.

- **Payor/Financer** – The party called on to respond financially. This can include the "transferee," an insurance carrier (as per insurance contract provisions) or some other financially responsible party (i.e. a sub-sub to whom financial responsibility has been contractually transferred).

There are three levels of contractual risk transfer.

- **Limited transfer**: The ***transferee*** only accepts the financial consequences of loss resulting from his sole negligence. If the transferor or another party contributes to the loss, the transferee is not financially responsible for that part of the loss. Essentially, the transferor is only protected for its vicarious liability arising out of the actions of the transferee.

- **Intermediate transfer**: The *transferee* agrees to accept the financial consequences of occurrences caused in whole or in part by its negligence. This includes if the transferor or another entity contributes to the loss in some way.

- **Broad transfer**: Provides the greatest scope and requires the transferee to indemnify and hold harmless the transferor from all liability arising out of an incident, even if the act is committed solely by the transferor. This may qualify as an ***exculpatory contract*** in some jurisdictions because such broad transfer is considered "unconscionable." Approximately 10 states allow the use of broad transfer, with a general requirement being that the transfer intentions be clear and unambiguous.

Legal professionals familiar with a particular jurisdiction must be consulted when comparing the level of transfer with the applicable state law. Each state stipulates the acceptable amount of transfer allowed via contract. Because of the potential differences between the requested contract and the legally allowed level of transfer, transferors often request additional insured status and a waiver of subrogation endorsement to assure they are protected should the contract violate the applicable law.

Indemnification, Hold Harmless and Waiver: The Heart of Contractual Risk Transfer

Effective contractual risk transfer requires specific wording in the contract between the transferor and the transferee. Commonly known as the "indemnity (or 'indemnification') agreement," many contracts contain some form of indemnification and hold harmless wording such as the following (only an example, not intended as legal advice):

- "For and in exchange for fair and equitable consideration, [transferee] (name of the lower tier party) agrees to indemnify, hold harmless and waive any right of subrogation against [transferor] (name of the upper tier party) from any and all liability or cost arising from bodily injury or property damage caused in whole or in party by the (transferee)."

Indemnity agreements are the heart of contractual risk transfer. "Indemnification" is the contractual obligation of one party (the transferee) to return another party (the transferor) to essentially the same financial condition enjoyed before the loss (without the improvement or betterment). Hold harmless wording shields the transferor from the effects of the legal liability that can be assigned to them as a result of the actions contractually transferred (based, to some extent, on the level of transfer jurisdictionally allowed).

Indemnification and hold harmless wording is not necessarily affected by, nor do they affect, the transferee's insurance coverage. It is purely a contractual issue requiring one party to stand in place of another – regardless of the presence of insurance to finance the costs. When insurance is lacking, the transferee holds two places, transferee and payor.

Waiver of subrogation is the third leg of many indemnification agreements (back to the rule of threes). Subrogation rights flow from the harmed party's rights to be made whole by the party responsible for the loss. If the right to recover from the transferor (the upper tier party) is contractually waived by the transferee prior to an injury, the transferee's (lower tier party's) insurer also has no right to subrogate. Waiver of subrogation should be solely addressed in the contract rather than endorsed to the CGL (although there are endorsements to accomplish this).

If a particular state's statute affects the level of indemnification allowed, waiver of subrogation wording may need to be addressed in a separate paragraph within the contract to lessen the chance that the provision will be voided if the level of transfer is outside of allowable transfer provisions.

Since the disparate financing and control techniques of insurance and contractual risk transfer are ultimately intertwined, understanding how each policy responds to contractual risk transfer language is paramount.

Conclusion

Nearly every insured enters into a contractual risk transfer agreement and assumes some amount of risk from another party. Such assumption can be by lease agreement, a maintenance agreement or a construction-related contract (the most often reviewed contractual language). Regardless of the source, contracts must be reviewed to ascertain the level of risk being transferred to the insured. The level of risk accepted must then be compared to the level of coverage provided by the subject policy. If the contractually accepted risk is broader than the coverage provided, the insured may be subject to a substantial out-of-pocket expense. Not every transfer is insurable.

Chapter 6

Understanding Negligence and Theories of Legal Liability

Negligence is the failure to act as a reasonable and prudent person would in similar circumstances. However, judgment regarding who is reasonable and prudent is often left in the hands of those who, themselves, are not reasonable and prudent – jurors. Although this last statement may be seen as an editorial comment, look at it from the perspective of a court room.

Plaintiff attorneys work to convince jurors that the defendant failed to act in a reasonable manner resulting in injury or damage to their client. Defense attorneys try to counter the argument. Plaintiff attorneys have emotion on their side and defense attorneys have only factual evidence to present.

What are the facts of legal liability? What is required for a person or entity to be considered "legally liable?" Factually, there are four parts to legal liability.

1. A duty to act or not act.
2. Failure to act or not act as required by the duty.
3. Injury or damage occurs.

4. Proximate cause. That is, an unbroken chain of events, with no superseding events between the failure to act and the injury or damage. If there are any intervening causes, negligence is questionable.

From an emotional standpoint, the jury "feels" for the person who was injured and puts themselves in the same place. The defendant generally has to depend on the "facts" of the case (as presented above). When the battle is between emotions and facts, the side depending on facts has a much more difficult fight.

Negligence Primer

Negligence theories apply differently throughout the country. Following is a discussion of negligence theories, some defenses and a couple of unique legal theories surrounding negligence and the resulting damage. Keep in mind, the state-specific information presented is current as of January 2010 and is subject to change.

Comparative Negligence: Each party's relative "fault" for the accident is compared and the injured party's (plaintiff) ultimate damages award is reduced by their percentage of culpability. For example, if the plaintiff is found to be 40% at fault, the $1,000 damages awarded would be reduced by $600. Three variations of the comparative fault rule are utilized. In each variation, the damaged party's award is reduced by the percentage of their own contribution to the incident.

- **Pure Comparative Fault**: Allows the damaged party to recover even if they are 99% at fault. Any award is reduced by their contribution to the injury or damage. Thirteen states apply this rule of comparative negligence: AK, AZ, CA, FL, KY, LA, MS, MO, NM, NY, RI, SD and WA.

- **Modified Comparative – 50% bar**: A damaged party cannot recover if they are 50% or more at fault. They are able to recover from 0% to 49% at fault. Twelve states apply this rule of comparative negligence: AR, CO, GA, ID, KS, ME, NE, ND, OK, TN, UT, WV.

- **Modified Comparative – 51% bar:** A damaged party can recover from another party provided they are no more than 50% at fault. Twenty-one states apply this version of comparative negligence: CT, DE, HI, IL, IN, IA, MA, MI, MN, NV, NH, NJ, OH, OR, PA, SC, TX VT, WI and WY.

Contributory Negligence: Application of the contributory negligence's common law doctrine states that if the injured person was even 1% culpable in causing or aggravating his own injury he is barred from any recovery from the other party. This is an absolute defense in the jurisdictions that apply this principle. Some jurisdictions require the defendant (the one "most at fault") to prove the negligence of the plaintiff (the one "most damaged"), while others required the plaintiff to disprove any negligence. Only five jurisdictions still apply pure contributory negligence: AL, DC, MD, NC and VA.

Last Clear Chance

A doctrine in tort law applicable in jurisdictions that subscribe to the contributory negligence of doctrine. Last clear chance allows a plaintiff that is contributorily negligent to recover if he is able to prove that the defendant (most at-fault party) had the last opportunity to avoid the accident. Essentially, the plaintiff's negligence is no longer part of the equation. The defendant had time and ability to prevent the accident and failed to take necessary action.

Restated in legalese: A showing, by the plaintiff, of something new and sequential which affords the defendant a fresh opportunity (of which the defendant fails to avail himself or herself) to avert the consequence of his original negligence.

There are four applicable categories of Last Clear Chance applied by the five remaining jurisdictions that utilize the contributory negligence rule.

- **Helpless plaintiff:** The plaintiff's initial negligence put him in a position from which he was powerless to escape by ordinary means. The defendant detects the danger with ample time to respond, but fails to act as a "reasonable" person would.
- **Inattentive plaintiff:** The plaintiff did not pay attention to his surroundings putting himself in

danger. The defendant discovers the peril and has time to respond, but fails to respond to avoid the accident.

- **Observant defendant:** The defendant actually sees the plaintiff in time to react and safely avoid the incident but negligently fails to respond as a reasonable person would.

- **Inattentive defendant:** The defendant simply fails to pay attention as a reasonable person should (cell phone is a good example) and is unable to respond to the plaintiff's helpless condition in time to avoid the accident.

Assumption of Risk (Volenti Non Fit Injuria): This is a defense against charges of negligence barring or severely limiting an individual's recovery under the tort of negligence. The defendant must prove that 1) the plaintiff was reasonably aware of and appreciated the danger involved, 2) the plaintiff voluntarily exposed himself to the danger, and 3) the assumed danger was the proximate cause of the injury or damage.

The first element of proving negligence is showing that a duty of care is owed. When one assumes the risk of an inherently dangerous or recognizably potentially dangerous activity, the duty of care is lifted off the individual or entity conducting the activity. With no required duty of care, there can be no negligence.

As stated, it must be proven that the assumed danger was the proximate cause of the injury or damage. A fan attending a baseball game recognizes the risk that he may be hit by a foul ball. Thus he has assumed the risk and the owner of the ball park does not have to take unreasonable steps to protect the fan against or to further warn of the possibility of being hit. However, the fan had no reason to expect a concession worker to get angry and hit him with a team flashlight. The assumed risk was not the proximate cause of the injury and the owner of the park can still be held negligent (vicariously).

Pure contributory negligence states (again, only five remain) use proven assumption of risk as a complete bar to recovery. Each ***comparative negligence*** state applies the assumption of risk defense differently.

- Some view it as a complete bar to recovery where an express written waiver is given by the injured party prior to the injury.
- Others apply "primary assumption of risk" barring recovery when a reasonable person voluntarily proceeds in the face of a known risk.
- Many simply apply the percentages of the assumption of risk against the ultimate damages award, thereby allowing recovery but reducing the amount of the award.

Special Legal Theories

Eggshell Skull: A legal term based in tort and criminal law that states that tortfeasors take the injured party as they find them. Also known as the "thin skull" rule, it states that if the injured party has a condition that predisposes them to greater injury than the normal human being, the tortfeasor is not relieved of any of the costs resulting from the bodily injury just because of the condition. All injury and the costs associated with such injuries are assigned to the individual that committed the initial wrongful act, regardless of the ability to foresee the results or the fact that the injury is made worse by a preexisting condition or predisposition to injury.

Crumbling Skull: A legal theory sometimes used as a defense to or argument against application of the "Eggshell Skull" rule. The principle behind this defense is that the result would have been the same whether or not the accused wrongdoer was involved. Best exampled in medical practices: the patient was dying, the doctor attempted some radical measures to maintain life and did not succeed and in fact were the proximate cause of death. Crumbling skull principles would not hold the doctor responsible for causing a foregone conclusion. To protect the doctor, the death would have to have been certain within approximately the same time frame.

Chapter 7

Using Coverage and Limits Gaps to Sell

Insureds depend on their agent for protection, but too many agents depend on prices to close the deal and "win" the client. Winning on price can be a Pyrrhic victory because making the "war" about price kills a majority of opportunities to establish a long-term relationship. Without a protection or risk management-based relationship, the agent will lose the client the same way he gained it – on price.

Insurance is not a commodity. Correctly designed protection in the wake of a major loss is the difference between the insured's utter financial destruction and its restoration to financial health. Agents are and must act like more than mere "order takers," they must be the professionals the protection they offer requires.

Becoming and practicing like a professional insurance agent necessitates analysis of the client's exposures and an understanding of the applicable insurance policy's limitations and exclusions. Checklists are the tools of insurance professionals. Their use confirms that all relevant questions are asked, but more importantly they reveal coverage gaps.

Checklists Win Clients

Every errors and omissions underwriter and loss control representative wants agents to use checklists. Agency consultants continually push the use of checklists. Agents, like the Grinch, imagine all the "noise" they are going to hear at the next E&O class about, you guessed it, checklists. But beyond the hyper-importance of protecting the agency in an E&O suit, checklists can actually help agents SELL MORE BUSINESS and MAKE MORE MONEY.

The "hassle" of using a checklist disappears when viewed from the perspective of increased income. But how do these annoying checklists help the agent sell more business? "Gaps" is the magic word; gaps in protection, gaps in the limits, all manner of gaps. In other words, checklists find the gaps that sell the client on the agent, allowing the agent to gain a new client and write more business.

Regardless of the coverage or client type, there are always gaps between the true exposure and the protection provided. Some gaps are purposed and others are a surprise to the client. It's the surprises the agent needs to discover, explain and win the client with. This is done with checklists.

Gaps lead to opportunities. The opportunity to unseat the incumbent agent; the opportunity to develop a strong agent/client relationship; and decreased likelihood the client will move solely due to a lower premium.

No More Talk of Checklists!

There is no more talk of checklists from this point forward, lest you tire of the conversation. The remainder of this chapter details the two classes of coverage/exposure gaps: 1) those that will almost certainly result in winning the client when presented, and 2) those that don't necessarily win the client but rather serve to cement the agent/client relationship.

Gaps Likely to get the Agent Hired (aka: "Type 1" Gaps)

"Type 1" gaps themselves fall into two subcategories: A) those common enough that a majority of insured within a particular class have the exposure; and B) gaps so uniquely situational and rare that only a very few insureds actually have the exposure. Both will win the client, but each requires a different approach.

"Common" coverage gaps ("Type 1.A." gaps) require skillful introduction and explanation. The mention of these gaps and their solutions should be conventional and not presented "checklist style."

"Checklist style" sounds like this. "Looking at my notes from our meeting, it appears that you have some unique exposures that we need to discuss," (the "notes" are, of course, the checklist that was completed). Don't misunderstand, the "checklist style" is not wrong, in fact this is the approach for "Type 1.B." gaps; but it is not the best approach for gaps common to a large percentage of insureds.

A conversational approach to coverage gaps is more effective because it is not necessarily required to first find out if the insured has the exposure. Most within a specific class do. The goal is to impart important information about these common gaps to the insured and then tell them how to fill the gaps.

Assume the insured owns a 20-year-old building. It's likely the building is not totally compliant with the current building code. The unendorsed commercial property policy does not respond to this exposure as it requires the attachment of the Ordinance or Law endorsement. Before meeting with the insured, the agent researches the jurisdictional building codes. At an appropriate place in the meeting (when the question regarding the age of the building is posed), the agent pauses and says "I was reviewing the local building codes and noticed that [name of jurisdiction] has some unusual requirements. If your building is damaged beyond 50% of its market value, it has to be torn down and rebuilt to current building codes. This could be costly."

Obviously the information presented to the client must be true and relevant. In the above example, the agent has the opportunity to explain the problem(s) (as there are multiple issues) and the solutions. Because most buildings within this "class" (more than 10 or 15 years old) don't meet building codes, the agent was able to plan ahead and proactively offer a solution (conversational style) rather than reactively find a solution (checklist style).

Conversational style doesn't look like or feel like selling. It's an exchange of information that builds trust. If the client is unconcerned with the exposure, it's still in the notes that the exposure was discussed. This style also moves the insured away from basing the decision on price alone.

Differentiating between "1.A." and "1.B." gaps is rather simple. While both are hot-button gaps that should convert a prospect into a client, "1.A." gaps are general in nature applying to all insured in a particular class (i.e. all homeowners' policies exclude personal injury, older buildings don't meet code, etc.) where "1.B." gaps are operational in nature. An operational gap is specific to the insured and is only known once the checklist is complete. The difference between the general nature and operational nature of these gaps gives rise to the different styles (conversational vs. checklist) used to discuss both.

Agents must look for, prepare for and capitalize on both of these client-winning gaps. Advanced preparation and policy knowledge are required.

Gaps that Cement Relationships (aka "Type 2" Gaps)

"Type 2" gaps are those that don't cause immediate panic or need in the insured, but those on which the insured wants to invest more time and discussion. Being able to act as a trusted authority and advisor allows the insured to build trust in the business relationship.

Common "type 2" gaps/exposures include coverage limits, valuation methods and contractual risk transfer issues. These, like the "1.B." gaps above, are nearly always operational exposures unique to the insured.

In the client's mind, these exposures/gaps do not require immediate attention, but they want the agent to invest time in researching the answers and offering alternatives.

Again, "type 2" gaps are not necessarily client winners (but they could be), they are relationship clenching. Addressing these issues will tie the client to the agent far better than price.

Synopsis

Use checklists to find gaps. Hot button gaps require preparation and study (agent has to know coverage and about the class of business being pursued). Capitalize on the gaps to win and tie yourself to the client for the long term.

Chapter 8

Understanding Commercial Property Underwriting and 'COPE'

Working nearly four years with the Commercial Risk Service division (now known as RDS) of Insurance Services Office (ISO) afforded me the opportunity to become somewhat well-versed in the recognition, gathering and reporting of the necessary property underwriting information known as "COPE" data.

Construction, **O**ccupancy, **P**rotection and **E**xposure (COPE) are the four basic elements of underwriting data real property underwriters have been using for nearly 300 years. Commercial property applications are designed to capture most of this basic underwriting data. Each element is discussed in more detail in the following paragraphs.

Construction ("C")

The construction element can be further broken down into three sub-parts. Each of the following sub-parts is detailed in the next several paragraphs.

- Construction materials
- Square footage
- Age of the structure

Construction materials

ISO defines six construction classifications (from "1" to "6") based on the combustibility and damageability of the materials used to construct the "major structural features" of a particular structure. The lower the number, the more susceptible the structure is to damage by fire (the main construction rating factor in this system). The "major structural features" used to determine the construction class codes are the exterior load-bearing walls, roof and floor(s).

Assigning a construction class code is first a function of the load-bearing wall material and secondarily a function of the floor and roof materials used. Four exterior, load-bearing wall types are considered: 1) masonry, 2) fire-resistive/modified fire-resistive, 3) non-masonry or fire resistive, and 4) combustible materials (wood). Likewise, there are four floor and roof types considered: 1) concrete, 2) modified fire resistive/fire resistive, 3) non-masonry or non-fire resistive, and 4) wood or materials other than "1," "2" or "3."

Combining one of the four wall types with one of the four floor/roof types produces the structure's construction class. Figure 8.1 illustrates how walls, floors and roof combine to generate a specific construction class. Only two universal "rules" apply to construction classifications: 1) if the exterior load-bearing wall is frame, the entire building is rated as frame (construction class "1"), regardless of the roof material; and 2) if the exterior load-bearing wall is anything OTHER THAN masonry, modified fire resistive or fire resistive, the structure's construction class based on the roof and floor construction material.

In applying this chart, remember that each "major structural feature" is often an assembly of several parts. When assessing one of these features, the entire assemblage creating that part must be considered and no "assembled" feature can be assigned a classification greater than its most combustible or susceptible part.

Two examples of "assemblages" lowering the structural feature's "class" are:

- An exterior metal-on-metal-stud wall with plywood or other combustible material attached to the inside of the wall (common in industrial settings). The combination of these two disparate materials requires that the entire section of wall covered with the combustible material be considered a combustible wall. If enough of the wall area is comprised of this assemblage, the entire wall, for rating purposes, may be considered frame.
- Wood joist roof supports covered with metal is considered a frame assemblage and is thus assigned a frame rating.

(The assembly rule, however, does not apply to load-bearing masonry, modified fire resistive or fire resistive walls.)

Beyond the six construction classes presented above and in the attached chart, there are actually three more construction classifications relating to Group II causes of loss (windstorm, hail, aircraft, riot, civil commotion, etc.). Construction class codes "7," "8" and "9" modify construction classes "2," "3" and "4" respectively. Agents will never use these three additional codes, just know that they exist and relate mostly to the structure's ability to withstand heavy wind loads.

Mixed Construction Problems. What affect does a combination of building materials and assemblies have on a commercial property's construction classification? Factually, such mixing can be detrimental to the building's construction class. From the attached chart it is evident that any building with a wall or wall assembly classified as frame results in the entire structure being rated as construction class "1" – frame, with some very expensive property rating results.

Simply, to qualify for a higher construction class rating, the superior construction must equal or exceed 66 2/3 % of the ratable structural feature. The 2/3 requirement applies first to the walls and separately to the combined area of the floors and roofs. (The lowest floor is not considered when calculating the total floor and roof area.)

Figure 8.2 gives two examples of mixed construction. The first is a one story building combining non-combustible and frame assembly walls all under a non-combustible roof. The second is a partial two story building with masonry walls a non-combustible roof and the second floor constructed of ¾ inch plywood on metal joists – making the second floor a combustible assembly.

Other Construction Material Considerations. In addition to the "major structural features" highlighted above, underwriters also review interior construction features that affect the damageability of the structure under consideration. Bowling alleys are a good example of this review. A rating charge is generally applied to bowling alleys due to the raised combustible floors making up the bowling lanes.

Square Footage

The size of a structure influences many aspects of the underwriting process related to the "construction" element of COPE. Structure size also plays a part in the "protection" section of COPE (i.e. the need for a sprinkler system, etc.). But the main aspect of structure size from the underwriting aspect is in the comparison of the building's "maximum possible loss" versus its "probable maximum loss."

"Maximum possible loss" (MPL) and "probable maximum loss" (PML) are concepts explored in Chapter 10, "How to Explain Coinsurance." Essentially it is **possible** that the entire structure may be destroyed in any one loss, thus the MPL is the entire structure. However, the chances that the building will suffer a total loss are inversely proportional to the size of the structure. Basically, the larger the building, the less likely the entire structure will be destroyed in a single event. The PML is a smaller percentage of the MPL in larger buildings.

Age of the Structure

Aging structures create concern and questions in the underwriter's mind. Specifically, underwriters will concern themselves with the building's major systems (roofing, plumbing, HVAC and wiring) when underwriting an older structure. The older the structure, the more likely a major system will malfunction, leading to a possible claim due mostly to an internal issue rather than caused by an external force.

Have the systems been maintained and updated as necessary? When were the last updates? What was the extent of those updates? Who did the updates? These are all questions underwriters may ask regarding older structures.

Agents should concern themselves with the age issue as well. Many construction-related ordinances and laws may have been updated or enacted since the building's original construction. Any increased cost related to bringing a structure into compliance with local building codes following a covered cause of loss is specifically excluded in the unendorsed commercial property policy.

The Importance of "Construction" Information

Taken on its own, "construction" may ultimately be the most important element in property underwriting. Although the second element, "occupancy" (what the insured does), is often seen as primarily important among the four elements, occupancy really is secondary to construction when the risk is a class of business the underwriter normally writes. Granted, construction and occupancy can each be seen as a function of the other in regard to underwriting decisions, often times the decision comes back to construction. For example, an underwriter may offer coverage to a restaurant in a masonry/non-combustible building (construction class "4"), but may not be willing to offer coverage to the same operation located in a joisted/masonry building (construction class "2").

Occupancy

"Occupancy" information is comprised of two parts: 1) what the insured does, and 2) how the insured manages the hazards associated with what they do. Determining what the insured does is rather simple. Determining how they manage their "hazards of occupancy" requires closer investigation (either by the agent, insurance carrier staff or independent inspection firm).

Each class of insured (retail, office, wholesale, manufacturing, service, etc.) presents its own relative risk of first party property loss. The greater the risk of loss, the more closely the underwriter analyzes the operations (occupancy) and the higher the relational cost of coverage. An office, for example, presents less of an operational hazard than does a paint and body shop, resulting in lower property occupancy rate factor for the office.

Beyond merely knowing the insured's operations/occupancy, the insurer must also investigate how the insured manages those operations (part two of the occupancy review). Similar insureds do not necessarily manage their operations similarly. Since each insured manages its exposures and hazards differently, each has its own "hazards of occupancy" that must be considered in the underwriting process.

Return to the paint and body shop referenced above as a "hazard of occupancy" example. Assume the underwriter is evaluating three separate shops; all three have similar construction, location and protection characteristics. However, each applies its own method of storing 150 gallons of flammable and combustible paint.

Shop "A" stores its paint in a non-vented, unapproved storage room within the building. Shop "B" stores all 150 gallons in several storage cabinets meeting NFPA 30 standards. Shop "C" stores all paint in an appropriately constructed storage building separate and apart from the shop. Which of these three presents the greatest (highest) hazard of occupancy? Which has the lowest relative hazard of occupancy?

All three shops will garner the same "occupancy" charge, but shop "A" will suffer the highest "hazard of occupancy" charge due to its storage methods. Shop "B" has mitigated its hazard by using approved containers and shop "C" has largely removed a common paint shop hazard of occupancy by choosing to store its flammable and combustible paints outside the building. The result is that shop "C" will likely have the lowest occupancy charge.

Paint storage is just one example of a hazard of occupancy. Underwriters should review all hazards of occupancy.

- Housekeeping (how neat and free of debris is the building and its surroundings)

- The amount of combustible materials within the building
- The condition of major systems (heating and wiring)
- Dust-collection systems for woodworking and like operations
- Use of spark-reduction equipment where necessary
- The amount of storage and any other potentially hazardous materials

Protection

Underwriters and building code officials are often jointly interested in the property protection aspects of structures, but for different reasons. Property underwriters view property protection measures in regards to their ability to lessen the amount of property damage. Building code officials generally view protection from a general public and personnel protection angle.

Sprinkler systems, fire extinguishers, alarm systems, fire doors and fire walls and public fire protection are the primary protection mechanisms evaluated by underwriters. A particular structure's construction and occupancy may dictate which property protection mechanisms are required or desired by the underwriters.

Sprinkler Systems

The mere presence of a sprinkler system is not, or should not be, sufficient to satisfy the underwriter. To be effective, the sprinkler system must meet the demands created by the hazards specific to the occupancy. A sprinkler designed for an office or warehouse will not provide sufficient protection to a chemical manufacturing operation. Insufficient systems are common when an existing building designed for one type of occupancy is later converted to another use (a warehouse is turned into a manufacturing facility).

Proper evaluation of a sprinkler system is generally done by a qualified professional. These inspectors evaluate the condition of the system and the ability of the system to handle the fire load created by the occupancy. Underwriters can glean important information from the inspector's report.

- The type of system (wet pipe, dry pipe, deluge, predation, etc.)
- Condition of the system (well maintained or any deficiencies)
- The system's ability to handle the fire load
- If the water supply is adequate for the occupancy
- If the location and number of sprinkler heads is adequate
- The size and location of any non-sprinklered area
- Whether there is adequate sprinkler protection in the situation where there is high-rack storage

Fire Extinguishers

Fire extinguishers, unlike a sprinkler system, require human interaction. To be effective, the extinguisher must be accessible, appropriate for the hazard and ready for use when needed. To garner maximum benefit from and credit for the presence of fire extinguishers, the underwriter should want to know the answers to several questions.

- Are there an appropriate number of fire extinguishers for the building?
- Are fire extinguishers properly located (travel distance no more than 75 feet from any point in the building) and at eye level?
- Are fire extinguishers in the path of natural exit (i.e. can the user access one on the way out of the building without having to put themselves in danger to obtain and use one)?
- Are fire extinguishers the correct size?
- Are the fire extinguishers the correct type?
  1. Class A – Paper, wood, etc.
     (anything that produces "A"sh)
  2. Class B – Flammable or combustible liquids
     (anything that "B"oils)
  3. Class C – Electrical fires
     (anything that has a "C"harge); and
  4. Class D- Combustible metals
     such as shaved magnesium.
- Are the fire extinguishers inspected and, if necessary, charged annually?

Alarm Systems

Fire, smoke, burglar and combination alarm systems are readily available to fit nearly any purpose or need. Before granting any credit or exception based on the presence of an alarm system, key information is required by the underwriter.

- Where does the alarm sound? Is it local only, or at an offsite location?
- If at an offsite location, is the monitoring company listed by Underwriters Laboratory (UL)?
- What type of external communication is used? (A digital or tape dialer)?
- What backup features does the system have?
- Are there any special protection features?
- Is the system installed properly?

The last question may seem rather simplistic, but planning an alarm system can be done incorrectly. Inspecting an alarm system in a restaurant on one occasion, the owner complained that the fire alarm often sounded (on and offsite) for no apparent reason). Upon investigation I found that a "rate-of-rise" detector had been installed over an oven. If the oven door was open long enough, the sudden rise in heat would set off the alarm. Proper installation of the system is important.

Fire Doors and Fire Walls

"Maximum possible loss" (MPL) and "probable maximum loss" (PML) are directly related to the presence and effectiveness of fire doors and fire walls. Properly constructed and maintained fire walls and doors limit the spread of fire and lower the PML. The lower the PML, the more favorably the underwriter views the property.

Large open buildings, based of course on the contents of the building, allow a fire the opportunity to spread rather quickly with nothing structural to slow the progress. Compartmentalized space created by fire walls and doors contain and slow the spread of fire to reduce the overall damage. At least that's the purpose of fire walls and doors.

To qualify as a fire wall (not just a "fire stop") requires certain conditions be met.

- The wall must be one continuous masonry wall.
- The wall must be at least 6 or 8 inches thick (based on the materials used).
- The wall must come into direct contact with fire resistive, masonry or noncombustible roofs.
- The wall must pierce "slow burning" or combustible (including assembly) roofs.
- If the exterior walls are masonry, fire resistive or non-combustible, the wall must be in direct contact with the walls.
- If the exterior walls are "slow burning" or combustible, the wall must pierce the exterior wall.

- If there is an opening in the wall, it must be protected by a self-closing "class A" (3-hour) fire door or a sprinkler curtain. Class "A" doors are only effective when they close as designed. If the door is blocked open or unable to fully close for any reason, the wall no longer qualifies as a fire wall.
- Any communications through the wall by HVAC ducts must be protected by at least one 1 ½ hour damper.

Any masonry or non-combustible wall failing to meet these standards is considered a "fire stop" but not a fire wall. Slow burning and combustible (including assembly) walls qualify as neither a fire wall nor a fire stop.

Public Protection

Fire districts, often involving many individual fire stations, are inspected and graded by Insurance Services Office or other jurisdictions with authority (in North Carolina, it's the Department of Insurance) based on response time, personnel, training, equipment and local water supply. Each district is assigned a number from 1 to 10. The lower the number the better the district and the lower the fire rate.

Exposures

Is the insured property exposed to any external hazards? Not all hazards are related to the insured structure or operation. Some come from outside the premises or are simply geographic in nature. Here are few external exposures relevant to property underwriters.

- The insured structure's proximity to a high-hazard operation
- The local wildfire risk
- The possibility for damaging winds and/or water
- The structure's flood zone location (located in or near a special flood hazard area (SFHA))
- The structures earthquake exposure
- The jurisdictions building code requirements

Finishing Up

Understanding COPE allows better planning during the property underwriting process. Knowing what specific information to provide (and why) makes the process smoother and hopefully quicker. Also, knowing COPE can assist clients when planning upgrades to current structures or constructing new buildings.

Construction Class Cheat Sheet
(Separated by Roof/Floor Material)

Exhibit 8.1

Wall Material	Floor/Roof Material	Construction Class	Code
Wood/Combustible	Wood/Combustible[1]	Frame	1
Non-Combustible/Metal	Wood/Combustible[1]	Frame	1
Masonry[2]	Wood/Combustible[1]	Joisted Masonry	2
MFR[3]	Wood/Combustible[1]	Joisted Masonry	2
FR[4]	Wood/Combustible[1]	Joisted Masonry	2

[1] Includes a "Combustible Assembly"
[2] One layer of non-load-bearing bricks covering metal studs is **not** considered a masonry wall.
   It is a combustible wall with a brick façade.
[3] Modified Fire Resistive
[4] Fire Resistive

Wall Material	Floor/Roof Material	Construction Class	Code
Wood/Combustible	Non-Combustible/Slow Burning[5]	Frame	1
Non-Combustible/Metal	Non-Combustible/Slow Burning	Non-Combustible	3
Masonry	Non-Combustible/Slow Burning	MNC[6]	4
MFR	Non-Combustible/Slow Burning	MNC	4
FR	Non-Combustible/Slow Burning	MNC	4

[5] This includes Built-Up Tar and Gravel Roof
[6] Masonry Non-Combustible

Wall Material	Floor/Roof Material	Construction Class	Code
Wood/Combustible	Concrete, MFR or FR	Frame	1
Non-Combustible/Metal	Concrete, MFR or FR	Non-Combustible	3
Masonry[7]	Concrete, MFR or FR	MFR	5
Masonry[8]	Concrete or FR	FR	6
MFR	Concrete, MFR or FR	MFR	5
FR[9]	MFR	MFR	5
FR	Concrete or FR	FR	6

[7] If the masonry does not meet the requirements of footnote "4" but is at least 4 inches thick, then the structure
   is classed as modified fire resistive.
[8] To qualify, the wall must be either: 1) **solid** masonry at least 4" thick; 2) hollow masonry at least 12" thick;
   3) hollow masonry between 8" and 12" thick with a listed fire resistance rating of at least 2 hrs.
[9] "Fire Resistive" is defined as a non-combustible material or assemblies with a fire resistance rating of at least
   2 hours. Can be accomplished based on the material or by the application of a sprayed on cementitious mixture
   covering all exposed metal. If between 1 and 2 hours fire resistance rating, the member is considered "modified
   fire resistive."

Example:
Differing Floor & Roof Materials

Exhibit 8.2

This structure was originally constructed as a one story, 3000 square foot (50'x60') structure with 12-inch masonry walls and non-combustible, built-up tar and gravel roof and a wall height of 20 feet. The building/business owner, due to the need for more storage area, added a 50'x30' mezzanine storage area over the front office area and extending into part of the work area. The storage area is ¾" plywood on top of metal joists – a combustible assembly. Prior to this addition, the building was rated as masonry non-combustible (construction class "4"). How does this addition affect the building's construction class? The answer is based on the combination of the floor and roof area since the exterior walls are all off the same masonry material.

Total Floor and Roof Area (50'x60')+(50'x30')	4,500 sq feet
Combustible Floor Area (50'x30')	1,500 sq feet (33.3%)
Non-Combustible Roof Area (50'x60')	3,000 sq feet (66.67%)

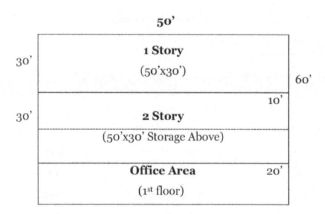

In this building, the construction class does not change. The reason: the superior non-combustible construction accounts for 66.67% of the combined roof and floor area. Thus the structure **retains its construction class "4" rating.** Had the second floor, combustible-assembly storage area been a greater percentage of the combined roof and floor area, the structure's construction classification would have to be changed to "2." Insured must be careful when making any additions.

Chapter 9

Understanding Insurance Property Values and Valuations

Replacement cost does not mean what the client believes or has been told. Insureds assume replacement cost translates into new stuff for old junk – because agents have told them that's how it works. Well, to be fair this is a partially true definition, but partially true definitions coupled with only partially met expectations can lead to wholly dissatisfied clients and a possible court date.

Property, real and personal, can have many "values," and replacement cost is only one possibility. Other values include how much it could bring on the open market, what an expert thinks it is worth, what it actually costs to replace and the value an individual places on the property. Not all of these relate to insurance or the application of insurance coverage.

Indemnification

Before any discussion of property values in insurance can commence, an understanding of the founding and guiding principal of property insurance must be established. Beginning with the earliest property policies, through the creation of the 165-line New York standard fire policy in 1918, up to property insurance policies of today, the goal of property insurance has been (and remains) the "indemnification" of the insured party.

Indemnification is the contractual obligation of one party (the indemnitor) to return another party (the indemnitee) to essentially the same financial condition enjoyed before the loss with no improvement or betterment. Property policies are two-party contracts (the insurer and the insured), where the insurer is the "indemnitor" and the "indemnitee" is the insured.

A key phrase in this definition is "...the same financial condition..." Insurance was not designed to improve the indemnitee's financial condition after a loss. Such improvement or enrichment would have the potential to create a moral hazard or a morale hazard.

Traditionally, indemnification has been a function of "the lesser of..." Meaning that the most the insured (indemnitee) will receive following a loss is the lesser of amounts specified in the policy. The commercial property policy, for instance, states the insurer's payment options.

- Pay the "value" of lost or damaged property.
- Pay the cost of repairing or replacing the lost or damaged property.
- Take all or any part of the property at an agreed or appraised value.
- Repair, rebuild or replace the property with other property of like kind and quality.

"Value" is initially defined in the property policy to mean "Actual Cash Value." Actual Cash Value (ACV) is the cost new less depreciation. A <u>simplified</u> application of ACV would be a 5-year-old piece of machinery with a 10 year useful life that is destroyed by fire. The ACV would be 50% of what a new machine would cost. The concept of ACV will be expounded upon in later paragraphs. The definition of "value" can be changed by choosing options already available in the policy, including replacement cost or agreed value.

Since the insurance carrier has the right to choose which of the four payment options will be used, payment will likely be limited to the least of these calculated amounts – unless there are laws or external circumstances that dictate the use of a different value or limit.

Broad Evidence Rule – External Circumstances

Some states require all external evidence surrounding the value of property be used to establish the true value or lack of value of insured property which is known as the Broad Evidence Rule. Application of the broad evidence rule can be to the insured's benefit, but in some cases its application can be detrimental to the insured when defining the value of property.

Insured's advantage: How does the insurer arrive at the 10 year useful life used in the ACV example above? Such calculations are usually derived from a chart or some other long-established method or computer program and based on averages. Such chart or program probably does not take into account any specialized maintenance or recent upgrades performed by the insured.

If the insured has performed routine plus extraordinary maintenance or upgrades, the example machine may actually have a useful life closer to 20 years. Without the application of the broad evidence rule, the insured could be out 25% of the value, that's $25,000 if the machine's replacement cost is $100,000.

Insured's detriment: Consider a recently purchased building slated for demolition. The land on which the building is located has all the value and the new owner has no need for the building. A demolition team has been scheduled to remove the building from the premises, but due to their schedule, it will be three months before demolition can begin. During that time, the owner begins removing fixtures and equipment, and turns off the power.

Because there is a loan on the property, the mortgagee requires a property insurance policy be purchased. Such policy is in full force on the day the building burns down. How much does the insurer owe for this building?

Case law in some states suggests that the insurer owes nothing because the building had no use and no real value to the insured. Since it was already slated to be torn down, the owner was benefited by "free" demolition. All the evidence surrounding the building and its value, the broad evidence, suggests the building is valueless. This is the other side of the broad evidence rule.

Now What!

What, then, is the definition and application of replacement cost, actual cash value, or even functional replacement cost? How does depreciation fit into insurance? Does everything depreciate? Is any of this affected by a faltering real estate market?

Replacement Cost Violates Indemnification

Assertion: Replacement cost violates the principle of indemnification because the insured is placed in a better position than existed immediately prior to the loss. For instance, the insured's five-year-old production machine is destroyed by a covered cause of loss and they get a new one in its place. This is an abuse of the insurance mechanism.

Point of Fact: Replacement cost is the ***truest*** form of property indemnification available. Consider it this way, the insured's machinery is destroyed by fire. Now the insured is missing the machinery. Money doesn't necessarily do any good; they need the equipment. The same idea applies to a building. The insured needs a building, not the money. Replacement cost is the best mechanism for returning the building and contents to the insured with the only out-of-pocket expense being the deductible chosen by the insured (provided limits have been chosen correctly). This is the best demonstration of the goal, purpose and representation of indemnification.

Still, how can replacement cost embody the principle of indemnification? Why is the insured not better off than before the loss? These are both valid questions which relate to the due diligence required to calculate the limits of property coverage.

Insurance to "Cost"

Indemnification principals are not violated and are, in fact, upheld because the amount of insurance purchased is intended to equal the cost new of all eligible and insured property on the day of the loss. To illustrate, the machinery involved in the loss exampled above cost $100,000 new five years ago. It has a current resale (market) value of $50,000, but to buy a new piece of equipment of like kind and quality today costs $150,000. When insuring on replacement cost basis, the only amount that matters is what it costs on the date of the loss. Thus, the insured would place $150,000 coverage on the machinery. The same process is applied to all real and personal property insured on a replacement cost basis to develop the true **insurance to cost** (ITC). Insurance to cost is equal to the current cost to buy or build another one like it (whatever "it" is) on the date of the loss.

Too often the level of calculation required to develop the true ITC is thumbed by the insured and even the agent. While it may not be reasonable to expect the insured or the agent to take time to calculate the cost new of every piece of machinery, equipment, furniture, stock or other covered property, this is the level of due diligence required to develop the correct replacement cost for contents. Insurers certainly apply this level of diligence when investigating and settling a property loss, particularly when confirming compliance with coinsurance provisions.

Insureds, or their agents, often just guess at the replacement cost of personal property. Guessing can create or heighten the coinsurance penalty. The coinsurance penalty and its relation to indemnification will be discussed in an upcoming chapter. One option is hiring an appraisal service to undertake this due diligence.

Developing an accurate replacement cost for the building is made much easier than precisely calculating the value of contents (business personal property) thanks to building cost estimators. Cost estimators coupled with knowledge of usual and customary square footage costs within the particular locale generally develop highly accurate insurance to value figures. But even this does not guarantee the insured will be paid their idea of replacement cost.

"Going Out of Business"

Insureds occasionally decide not to rebuild or replace lost property after a loss and instead elect to go out of business. Property policy provisions guard against violating the principal of indemnification if an insured makes this decision. Insureds choosing not to rebuild or return to previous operations will receive the property's actual cash value. The principal of indemnification remains intact because the insured gets no more than the remaining value of the insured property – the remaining (cash) value of what they lost.

Indemnification is accomplished when the insured is returned to essentially the same financial condition that existed prior to the loss. Replacement cost accomplishes this by providing the insured a fully furnished and equipped operation and no better. If the insured chooses not to reopen the business, they are out 'nothing' (they don't need the building and/or its contents any more) and are essentially made whole by being paid the remaining use value (depreciated value) of what they had.

Defined Values

Three distinctly different property "values" were used in the above paragraphs: actual cash value, replacement cost and market value. Two are common to insurance, and one generally has no relevance in insurance, until the government gets involved.

Actual cash value (ACV) is the initial valuation method applied in the commercial property policy. Even if the replacement cost option is chosen, some property continues to be valued at ACV. Actual cash value is defined as the cost new (replacement cost) on the date of the loss minus physical depreciation. "Physical" is highlighted because there are many different types of depreciation such as depreciation due to obsolescence, accounting depreciation and economic depreciation. None of these relate to the insurance definition of depreciation. Physical depreciation results from use and ultimate wear and tear meaning that the insured does not get paid for the "used up" value of the property.

Attention must be paid to the beginning point in the calculation of ACV, the cost new on the date of the loss. ACV is not based on the value when it was purchased or at any point between that date and the date of the loss. The cost new on the date of the loss is the figure that matters. This is key when choosing limits, the insured must still calculate the cost new even if using ACV as the loss settlement option.

Replacement cost was defined above, the cost to replace property with property of like kind and quality on the date of the loss. There is no allowance or penalty for age, depreciation or condition. The insured must simply insure the property at what it will cost to buy or build it today.

Market value is what a willing buyer will pay a willing seller on the open market. It is not normally a value with any relationship to insurance. The rise and fall of the market value does not necessarily change the cost to rebuild a building following a loss.

Understanding that this discussion mainly revolves around commercial property, the housing market is still a good example of this point. In 2008, there was a major decline in real estate values. Census department statistics state that the average value of a home fell 11.2 % from March 2007 to March 2008 and the National Association of Realtors reported that 2007 saw a 7.68 % decrease in housing prices. Does this mean that the cost to rebuild a particular house has changed? No! It simply means the person could not sell it for as much as they could a year ago. However, it would still cost the same (or even more) to rebuild the same house if it burned down.

Market value has nothing necessarily to do with insurance value, except in ordinance or law issues and flood coverage.

Replacement Cost not always 'Replacement'

Replacement cost is an optional valuation method within the commercial property policy activated by checking the right box on the application. It is, however, the "standard" valuation clause applied to eligible property in Businessowners' Policy (BOP). Even when this option is chosen, the insured does not automatically receive the replacement cost, as they understand it, for several reasons.

1. Replacement cost is not paid until the property is repaired or replaced.
2. Some types of property are limited by policy provisions and do not qualify for replacement cost, or are limited in the amount of coverage under replacement cost.
3. If the insured does a poor job calculating the limits, a coinsurance penalty could be applied.
4. "Replacement cost" does not necessarily guarantee payment for the ultimate cost to rebuild.

Ineligible for Replacement Cost

Property not contractually eligible for replacement cost includes: personal property of others; contents of residence (remember this is a discussion of the commercial property policy); works of art, antiques or rare articles, including etchings, pictures, statuary, marbles, bronzes, porcelains and bric-a-brac; and "stock." Loss to these types of property is settled at actual cash value. But two of these classes of property can be changed to replacement cost if indicated in the application and shown on the declarations page.

Bric-a-brac is defined in the American Heritage Dictionary and other sources as "small articles, usually ornamental in nature, valuable due to their antiquity, rarity, originality or sentimental nature." The term carries with it the idea of obsolescence – receiving the cost new for an obsolete article would be a violation of indemnification and the broad evidence rule. In addition to being potentially obsolete, this type of property as well as antiques, artwork, etc. may not be replaceable at any price, thus the insurance carrier is unwilling to extend replacement cost coverage to these types of articles.

Replacement Cost Optional

Stock and personal property of others can be valued on a replacement cost basis rather than ACV by indicating that desire on the application. Insureds having a large amount of personal property of others should consider this extension for two reasons: avoiding good will problems with clients, and to satisfy any contractual or legal requirements.

Valuing stock at replacement cost is a function of the circumstances and rarely do the circumstances necessitate the use of the replacement cost option. Stock subject to very quick turnover or with very little fluctuation in value likely does not need to be valued at replacement cost as there is no real depreciation. Even products with a long shelf life or greatly fluctuating values may not require replacement cost valuation.

Remember, actual cash value is defined as the cost new on the date of the loss less physical depreciation. Since the products are not being used, there is no physical depreciation, allowing the insured to essentially get replacement cost on stock anyway. Actual cash value may be the preferred valuation method for stock provided correct limits are maintained, especially in situations where values fluctuate greatly (there are two other options for insuring property that experiences great fluctuation in value).

Limited Replacement Cost

Several specific classes of property are valued at replacement cost, but are limited in the amount of coverage available. Classes include, but are not limited to, outdoor property, property off premises and outdoor sings attached to the building. One property within this classification severely limited by its "condition" is vacant property. Vacancy is defined in the commercial property policy, along with the coverage penalty for vacancy. The insured may believe that they will be paid replacement cost, but the policy states that any loss payment will be reduced by 15% (and some causes of loss that might have otherwise been covered are specifically excluded). This policy provision needs to be clearly addressed with the client, should the agent learn that an insured property is vacant.

Coinsurance – Everyone's Favorite

A third barrier to receiving the full replacement cost is the coinsurance provision. Coinsurance was created to assure that the insurance carrier would receive adequate premium for the risk being insured. Without this penalty, an insured might be persuaded to buy a small amount of coverage on a large building because of the difference between ***maximum possible loss*** and ***maximum probable loss***.

The maximum <u>possible</u> loss of any structure is the entire building, but depending on the construction and fire protection the maximum <u>probable</u> loss might be only half the building. Without the coinsurance requirement, insureds might be tempted to purchase coverage equaling only 50 % of the value of the building. The insured would be fully compensated for all losses falling under that amount and statistically, most losses would fall within these parameters.

Coinsurance provisions were created to eliminate this practice and to penalize insureds that fail to adequately insure their property. In effect, violators of the provision become co-insurers of the property. They self-insure part of the loss.

Insureds failing to meet coinsurance requirements are once again subject to the problem of "lessor of." If the limits of insurance purchased do not equal or exceed the value of the insured property on the date of loss (regardless of the valuation method chosen (ACV or replacement cost)) multiplied by the coinsurance percentage shown, the insured receives the <u>lesser of</u>: 1) the amount of insurance purchased, or

2) the result of the coinsurance calculation, both minus the applicable deductible.

The following chapter, "How to Explain Coinsurance" provides a more detailed explanation of these concepts.

The Government Strikes Again

Jurisdictional involvement is the fourth barrier alluded to above. Insureds believe, because it is what they have been taught, that replacement cost means new for old. It does, but not when exclusions intervene.

Following a covered cause of loss, the unendorsed property policy written on a replacement cost basis will pay exactly that, the cost to replace the damaged property – but no more. This policy will pay to rebuild the building exactly as it stood. Any additional cost necessary to bring the building up to current building code will be borne by the insured.

Having to explain this to the insured is tough enough. Try explaining that the cost of tearing down the undamaged portion of the building to allow the entire building to be brought up to current building code is not covered by the policy, even though the policy is written on replacement cost.

These additional costs are covered by the ordinance or law endorsement.

Ordinance or Law – When Government Strikes!

Ordinance or law endorsements fill a major gap between the insured's belief about replacement cost and the commercial property policy's actual application of this valuation method. Disparity between the insured's concept and the true operation of replacement cost often arises from the development, codification and enforcement of building codes.

Building ordinances and laws are enforced by local jurisdictions but the codes are promulgated by an assortment of contributors including state government, federal codes and regulations and advisory organizations such as the National Fire Protection Association (NFPA). States use these sources to create the statutory infrastructure but endow local jurisdictions with the authority to adopt and customize building codes to meet local preferences as needed.

Specific legal requirements stipulate the point at which a structure must be brought in compliance with local building codes. Correction of life safety issues presenting imminent danger is generally required immediately regardless of surrounding circumstances. Otherwise existing structures are generally granted "grandfather" status and are not required to comply with the applicable building codes unless certain statutorily specified events occur. "Major damage" to the building is one of those qualifying events.

Major damage does not have a universal definition. Each jurisdiction establishes and applies its own meaning. There are, however, two broad categories of major damage into which most state and local buildings fall.

- ***The Jurisdictional Authority Rule:*** States using this as the measure of major damage allow the authority having jurisdiction (the local government) to judge when a damaged building must be brought into compliance with the current building code.

- ***The Percentage Rule:*** When a building is damaged beyond a certain percentage of its "value," the entire structure must be brought into compliance with local building code.

When government has the opportunity (or feels the need) to inject itself into issues related to property values, problems erupt as evidenced by these rules. Both rules present unique problems regarding insurance coverage and common policy provisions.

The jurisdictional authority rule is subjective in its application. Each jurisdiction applies its own standard to define major damage and determine a structure's fitness for continued use. Decisions can be based on the amount of damage, the age of the building coupled with pre-loss compliance shortfalls or simple safety concerns. There is no one criterion upon which building owners and agents can depend, making risk management and insurance planning very difficult in these states.

Even the percentage rule's definition of "value" differs in the amount in states that apply this rule. "Value" could mean actual cash value, appraised value or market value.

Market value is negotiated between (and agreed to by) a willing buyer and a willing seller. It can fluctuate up and down based on the economy, condition, use or need and has little relation to the true cost to rebuild a particular structure.

However, if market value is the rule applied, the agent must be prepared for and be able to explain this concept.

Agents must know which rule of "major damage" is applied and how the individual jurisdictions apply the rule. Knowing this, the agent can explain the exposure and how replacement cost in the unendorsed property policy will and will not respond to losses triggering jurisdictional ordinances or law requirements.

Three Ordinance or Law Coverage Parts

Replacement cost alone falls short of paying much of the additional costs necessitated by a major loss (as defined above and by the applicable law). Damage crossing the threshold of "major" effectively creates a constructive **total loss** of the structure. However, the unendorsed commercial property policy only pays to repair or replace the damaged property back to the condition that existed prior to the loss.

No coverage exists in the unendorsed policy to pay the loss in value of the undamaged portion of the building no longer useable (the insured loses the use and value of the undamaged part). The cost to tear down and remove the undamaged portion of the building from the site is also borne by the insured. Finally, the additional cost necessary to bring the building into compliance with the current building code is wholly paid from the insured's financial resources.

When Ordinance or Law coverage is endorsed to the commercial property policy, it assures the insured is indemnified (put back into the same condition enjoyed before the loss) for the expenses which would otherwise be out-of-pocket. The endorsement's three coverage parts close the commercial property policy gaps highlighted above.

- ***Coverage A – Loss to the Undamaged Portion of the Building:*** The remaining portion of the building cannot be used due to application of the local building code. The insured is out the use value of this section making the building a constructive total loss. This coverage part pays that loss of value.

- ***Coverage B – Demolition Cost:*** Once the undamaged portion of the building has been torn down it must be removed from the site. The commercial property policy only pays to remove damaged property, Coverage B pays the cost to tear down and remove the undamaged part of the building.

- ***Coverage C – Increased Cost of Construction:*** All buildings must be built in compliance with applicable building codes. Buildings that suffer major damage are no exception. Replacement cost coverage only pays to put back what was there. This coverage part pays the additional cost necessary to bring the building into full compliance with current building codes.

Ordinance or Law coverage also fills the gap between the insured's belief about replacement cost and its customary application. Insureds must be informed of the exposures faced and the solutions available.

Building codes change and are updated frequently. The insured's building can become non-compliant very quickly. Most commercial properties over five years old fail to meet current building codes. Major damage triggering the application of the jurisdiction's laws or ordinances has the potential to cost the insured a large amount of out of pocket expense if the correct coverage is not provided, and the older the building is, the more expensive this gap in coverage is.

Property Value Options

Property insurance valuation options are not limited to replacement cost, actual cash value or even market value (although market value is not a customary insurance valuation). Insureds can choose among several specialized options to meet specific needs: functional replacement cost, agreed amount and stated value. Each valuation method has a specific use and meets a unique need as highlighted in the next several paragraphs.

Functional Replacement Cost

Building codes may not allow, or the realistic needs of the insured may not require, that a building be rebuilt to the same square footage or utilizing the same materials existing prior to a major loss. Likewise, the insured may not need furniture, fixtures or equipment with a myriad of additional features. ISO offers two endorsements which allow insureds to value real and personal property at less than replacement cost, but in amounts adequate to rebuild or replace with property that is operationally equivalent.

- CP 04 38 – Functional Building Valuation
- CP 04 39 – Functional Personal Property Valuation – Other Than Stock

Functional replacement cost endorsements value property at the cost necessary to replace damaged or destroyed property with new property of <u>unlike</u> kind and quality which perform the same general function allowing the insured to accomplish their business objectives. Property replaced using functionally equivalent materials and products are less expensive and often require a shorter replacement schedule. Buildings may be smaller or built using less expensive building materials and business personal property will perform the essential functions, but may not have the amenities of the furniture or equipment it replaces. There are times when this valuation option may be appropriate.

- The insured cannot rebuild the same square footage, usually due to the application of building codes, and a smaller building will be built in its place
- The insured does not want to rebuild the same square footage.
- Lower cost building materials can or should be used (i.e. masonry/non-combustible vs. fire resistive).
- The insured does not need all the functions available on a particular piece of machinery or equipment (they

found a great bargain on a top-of-the-line model, but don't need or use all the functions available and the insured does not want to pay the premium to insure it to replacement cost).

Both functional replacement cost endorsements allow the insured to purchase a lower amount of coverage (enjoying some premium savings) while remaining a **form** of replacement cost coverage for partial losses (subject to "lesser of" policy provisions). Other advantages within these forms include: 1) Coinsurance is waived, and 2) Ordinance or Law coverage is included in the form (no need for a separate endorsement.

Agreed Value

As the name suggests, this is the amount the insured and the insurer agree the property is worth. Since it is a "pre-negotiated" limit, the coinsurance condition does not apply provided the insured carries the amount of coverage agreed upon by both parties. The face amount is paid in the event of a total loss and partial losses are paid on a repair or replacement basis without the customary "lesser of" conditions common to other valuation methods.

Commercial property policies contain agreed value language. To trigger coverage the insured must 1) request the agreed value option in the application, and 2) complete and sign a statement of values for the insurance company to prove the values. The statement of values must be completed every

12 months in order to maintain agreed value coverage. If the statement of values is not completed, the coinsurance condition is reinstated.

Agreed value is appropriate anytime the insured wants to avoid potential coinsurance penalties. Such problems may arise when property is difficult to value due to its unique nature, availability or unstable values (which may trigger value and coinsurance issues as the cost at the time of loss may not be predictable). Retail or manufacturing operations which experience broad swings in stock value should avoid agreed value coverage on stock as limits may not be adequate to amount on hand at the time of loss.

Stated Amount

Stated amount is often times confused with agreed value when discussing and planning coverage with the insured. These terms are not synonymous. In fact, stated amount valuation is detrimental to the insured as it is wholly subject to the "lesser of" limitation with no option available to increase payment.

Most often applied in inland marine policies and auto physical damage coverage, stated amount will only pay the lessor of the state amount on the policy, the actual cash value, or the cost to repair the item.

There is rarely a situation where this valuation method is advantageous to the insured. Stated amount endorsements should be avoided and every attempt should be made to negotiate a different settlement option in policies that apply this as the primary valuation method (mostly inland marine coverage). If the only way an underwriter will agree to write the coverage is use of the stated value method and there are no other viable options, then the provisions must be clearly explained to the insured.

Coinsurance and Inflation Guard

Coinsurance provisions, requirements and penalties were addressed in an earlier section. Not discussed were the available coinsurance options along with the benefits and pitfalls of each. Remember, coinsurance was introduced to penalize the insured that failed to purchase a required minimum amount of property coverage.

The standard commercial property coinsurance percentage is 80%. That is, the insured must insure to at least 80% of the property's "value" to receive full payment for partial loss. "Value" is either actual cash value or replacement cost value based on the insured's indicated desire in the application. 90% and 100% are the two other common coinsurance percentages used in property policies.

Rate credits are granted when the insured increases the property policy's coinsurance percentage. However, when the coinsurance percentage is increased, the insured must confirm that the limits of coverage correspond to the new "minimum" limit of protection. The potential of suffering a coinsurance penalty increases as the insured increases the coinsurance percentage. If the insured opts to use 100% coinsurance, they must be absolutely sure that the limit of coverage equals 100%

of the "value" (however defined) to avoid a coinsurance penalty. Opinions differ, but the rate credit is not worth the potential penalty for miscalculation.

Insure the property at 100% insurance to value (again, whichever definition of value is applied), but use 90% coinsurance as the basis. This accomplishes two goals: 1) guarantees that the insured is fully insured for all partial losses (subject to the deductible); and 2) assures the insured will be fully covered for total losses since the policy will never pay more than the limit purchased.

Agents and insureds that insist on using 100% coinsurance do have an optional coverage to allow the property limit to increase throughout the year. The optional inflation guard coverage increases the limit of coverage over the course of the policy year. Coverage is increased by the percentage selected by the insured when this option is chosen. Annual inflation factors generally range between 2% and 8% and are prorated throughout the year (i.e. after six months, property values have been increased by one-half of the factor applied). Using 8%, property valued at $100,000 at the beginning of the policy period will be valued at $108,000 at the end of the 12-month policy period.

The inflation guard optional coverage is useful when the insured insists on 100% coinsurance or in volatile economic times.

Conclusion

Property has many different values. Some relate to insurance and many do not. Accurately valuing property for insurance, and even market, purposes is as much an art as a science. Insureds depend on their agents to protect them against devastating financial consequences following a loss. If the correct amount or the right type of coverage is not there, insureds can be bankrupted by the costs.

Insureds must understand the definition of "value," how to calculate the correct "value" and how policy provisions truly apply. Coverage gaps and solutions to close those holes must also be explained to insureds.

Chapter 10
How to Explain Coinsurance

Coinsurance provisions found in property policies exist primarily to assure that the insurance carrier receives adequate premium for the risk insured. Without a coinsurance condition, and its applicable penalties, insureds might be willing to purchase an amount of coverage somewhat less than the value of the subject property because of the statistically low probability of a total loss. The purchase of lower limits lowers the collectable premium which ultimately necessitates higher rates.

"Maximum" Losses

Property is subject to two types of loss "maximums" which can lead to the discrepancy between insurable value and the insurance carried as alluded to in the first paragraph: 1) Maximum <u>Possible</u> Loss (MPL) and 2) <u>Probable</u> Maximum Loss (PML). The key terms are "**possible**" and "**probable**."

It is "possible" that the entire structure may be destroyed in any one loss, thus the MPL is the entire value of the structure – the Total Insurable Value (TIV). However, a partial loss is statistically more likely than a total loss, thus the amount of the expected loss is considered the structure's "probable" loss.

A structure's PML is based on several factors: its construction, the occupancy and the protections against losses employed in the insured structure. These are three of the four **COPE** factors property underwriters use in making coverage and pricing decisions ("exposure" is fourth).

For example, a match manufacturing operation within a frame building (construction class 1) with no sprinkler system and located within a public protection class 9 fire district is far more likely to suffer a nearly maximum loss than is a fully sprinklered, modified fire resistive (construction class 5) office building in a public protection class 3 community. The PML of the match manufacturing operation closely approximates and may even equal its MPL; whereas the PML (again, the probable maximum loss) of the office building is likely closer to 40 or 50% of the MPL. To clarify, the match manufacturer is likely to burn completely to the ground, while the maximum expected fire loss to the described office may be limited to only half of the building.

Insureds with the greatest difference between the PML and MPL, lacking the coinsurance provision, might only purchase enough property protection to cover its anticipated PML. In the case of the office building, the insured might only purchase 50% of the TIV since that is all they expect to be damaged or destroyed in the worst expected loss. A degree in engineering or fire science is not necessary to judge the potential fire loss or threat posed by other perils, so the insured can arrive at the same conclusions.

The insurance industry realized this potential (some carriers may have even been victimized by such practices) and in the late 1800's to early 1900's created the (now) common coinsurance condition. Insureds are encouraged to insure a very high percentage of the structure's total insurable value. Such requirement allows property insurers to apply adequate yet not excessive rates.

What Does All That Have to Do with Clients

A majority of clients are probably not interested in MPL's, PML's or statistics, so explaining the computations and risks underlying coinsurance may not be necessary (or even wanted). But having the necessary background information allows the agent to better relate to the client that the coinsurance condition is not of itself a penalty. Rather it's a claims payment and rating provision allowing insurers to keep property rates lower than they otherwise could if insureds were allowed to purchase whatever amount of coverage they wanted without penalty, regardless of the total insurable value of the structure being protected.

But even this universal coinsurance truth is nebulous to the insured. The insured simply wants to know what is required to avoid the coinsurance penalty and how their coverage and ultimate loss payment is affected by the requirement.

Simply Put

Coinsurance provisions found in property policies require the insured to purchase **and maintain** some percentage of the structures TIV. The most common requirement is 80% of the structure's TIV at the time of the loss. This means that if the insured structure's TIV is $100,000 and there is an 80% coinsurance requirement, the insured must carry $80,000 of coverage to receive full payment for a partial loss (less any deductible).

The **simplified** final coinsurance calculation is:

- **Did/Should x Loss – Deductible = Payment**

"Did" (also known as Amount Carried) is easy to decipher, that is the amount of coverage the insured actually purchased. "Should," the Amount of Coverage Required ACR, is the product of two factors: 1) the TIV of the property at the time of the loss and 2) the coinsurance percentage required by the policy.

The "Should" calculation is:

- **TIV x Coinsurance Percentage = Should**

"Should" for a structure with TIV of $500,000 and policy coinsurance requirement of 80% is $400,000 (TIV x 80%). Be careful to not misconstrue the term "should." It does not and cannot be understood to mean the maximum amount of insurance coverage that should be carried. It simply indicates the minimum amount that must be carried to assure full payment of all partial losses (less any deductible).

Applying all applicable factors, the initial coinsurance calculation looks like this:

- **((Did/ (TIV x Coinsurance Percentage)) x Loss) – Deductible = Payment**

Insureds lacking adequate limits of coverage ***at the time of the loss*** are subject to the penalty prescribed by the condition. In effect, the insured becomes a "co-insurer" of the loss because they have chosen to carry less than the contractually-required amount of coverage (thus the term, "coinsurance"). Example 10.1 highlights the application of this calculation.

Notice that to be fully insured for partial losses, the insured in the attached example must carry at least $400,000. Adequate limits assure that the insured will not participate as a co-insurer in any partial loss. However, this is true only of partial losses. Even if the example insured purchases $400,000 in coverage, fully meeting the coinsurance requirements spelled out in the policy, it is still underinsured for a total loss. An insured will not be paid more than the applicable limits of coverage purchased, so if the entire building is destroyed, the maximum the insured in the attached example will receive is $400,000 and is underinsured by $100,000.

Following

Describing and calculating the coinsurance provision and "penalty" is the simple part. The next chapter details the unique features of coinsurance and discusses the differences between the commercial property policy's application of the coinsurance provision and the homeowners' policy's use of this policy condition.

Coinsurance Calculation Examples **Exhibit 10.1**

Insured Property Information

Total Insured Value (TIV):	$500,000
Coinsurance Required:	80%
Deductible:	$1,000
Amount of Loss:	$50,000

Inadequate Limits of Coverage

Amount of Insurance Carried – "Did"	$350,000
Amount of Insurance Required (TIV x Coinsurance) – "Should" ($500,000 x 80%)	$400,000
Coinsurance Penalty Calculation Factors 1. Did/Should ($350,000/$400,000) 2. Loss Amount 3. Deductible	1. 0.875 2. $50,000 3. 1,000
Coinsurance Penalty Calculation: (1. X 2.) – 3.	(0.875 x $50k) - $1,000
Amount of Payment (From Coinsurance Penalty Calculation Above)	$42,750
Amount of Coinsurance Penalty (Ignoring Deductibles) (Loss Amount – Payment Amount (before deductible)) $50,000 - $43,750	$6,250

The insured is a "co-insurer" on this loss in the amount of $6,250. For all partial losses, the insured is only going to be paid 87.5% of the damage amount prior to the application of the deductible. Had the loss been $100,000, the insured would be paid ((0.875 x $100,000)-Deductible) which totals $86,500. Again, the insured would be a co-insurer in the amount of $12,500 for the loss. To be fully insured for partial losses in this example, the insured msut carry at least $400,000.

Chapter 11

The Differences between the Application of Coinsurance in Homeowners' and Commercial Property Policies

Commercial property policies (CPP's) and homeowners' forms widely differ in the application of the coinsurance condition. The coinsurance calculation is the same, but little else applies to both coverage types.

What is the "Total Insurable Value" (TIV)

Property has many different values: replacement cost, actual cash value, market value, tax value, and even accounting value among others.

Replacement cost and actual cash value (ACV) are the only two property values to be considered when developing and choosing the limits of property coverage and applying the coinsurance penalty. None of the other named property "values" relate specifically to insurance ("market value" does play a part in <u>ordinance or law</u> losses and <u>flood</u> losses, but should not be considered otherwise).

Homeowners' policies value most real property (Coverages "A" and "B") at replacement cost (unless altered by the HO 04 81 ACV endorsement). So for Coverages "A" and "B," TIV is based on the property's replacement cost at the time of the loss. If the amount of coverage does not equal or exceed the **replacement cost** TIV multiplied by the coinsurance percentage, the insured will not be fully covered for partial losses.

Commercial property policies (CPP's) in contrast may use either ACV or replacement cost depending on the options chosen by the insured when the policy is first placed. Unaltered CPP's value real and personal property at ACV; the insured must specifically request the replacement cost settlement option. The basics of the coinsurance calculation are the same regardless of the valuation method chosen; the difference is in the values used to calculate the coinsurance penalty. If the insured alters the CPP by choosing replacement cost, it must confirm that all the values are correct and current to avoid application of the coinsurance penalty.

Many published discussions of coinsurance speak of the up and down values of commercial and residential structures and the need to stay on top of values to assure that the coinsurance condition is satisfied. Sadly, these discussions are confusing replacement cost and actual cash value with market value. Market values (what a willing buyer will pay a willing seller) do fluctuate, but replacement cost and ACV don't see wide variations from year to year. An exception to this statement occurs in the aftermath of a catastrophe when the cost to rebuild a structure steeply increases because demand for labor and materials far surpasses the supply.

What Property is Subject to Coinsurance?

Homeowners' and commercial property policies also differ in regards to the types of property to which the coinsurance condition applies. The Insurance Services Office's (ISO) homeowners' policy limits the applicability of coinsurance to only real property losses – Coverages "A" and "B." This is even true of ISO's dwelling property program. However, coinsurance applies to all "covered property" in ISO's commercial property policy. This includes both real and business personal property.

Condition "C" – Loss Settlement in the HO-3 states that buildings covered under Coverage "A" and "B" are valued at replacement cost (as discussed above), subject to an 80% insurance-to-value (ITV) requirement. The policy goes on to describe the coinsurance calculations as detailed earlier, but the homeowners' policy does not give a coinsurance calculation example.

In contrast, the additional condition "coinsurance" ("F.1.") in ISO's commercial property policy states that the coinsurance condition applies to real and personal property as follows:

"We will not pay the full amount of any loss if the value of Covered Property at the time of loss times the Coinsurance percentage shown for it in the Declarations is greater than the Limit of Insurance for the property."

"Covered property" is defined at the outset of the CPP as building ("A.1.a."), business personal property ("A.1.b.") and personal property of others ("A.1.c"). The coinsurance condition applies to each of these classes of covered property. The interesting part is that the insured could be adequately insured for one class of property yet underinsured on another.

Note also the difference in the location of the specified coinsurance percentage. The homeowners' policy specifies 80 % in the coverage form itself (but it can be altered by the HO 04 56 Special Loss Settlement endorsement). The CPP refers the reader to the declaration page to find the applicable coinsurance percentage. 80% is the traditional amount, but it is not the only percentage available for commercial property, as is discussed in an upcoming section.

Differences in Applying Coinsurance (Not Always a Penalty)

Another difference between the coinsurance conditions contained in the commercial property policy and homeowners' form is in the application of coinsurance as a penalty related to the final loss payment. CPP provisions penalize violations of coinsurance provisions, but the homeowners' form indemnifies the insured even when the coinsurance requirement test is failed.

Once determined that the insured did not carry enough protection to satisfy the coinsurance provision, the **CPP** mandates that the coinsurance penalty calculation be completed. Once calculated, the insured gets paid the **LESSER** of: 1) the limits of insurance, or 2) the results of the coinsurance calculation.

ISO's homeowners' policy does not necessarily apply the coinsurance calculation as a punishment. Indemnification is still preserved in the policy wording. While the opportunity for the structure to be covered at replacement cost is deleted, the policy still states that if the insured fails to maintain adequate insurance, the insured will be paid the **GREATER** of: 1) the damaged property's actual cash value, or 2) the results of the coinsurance calculation (both subject to the limits of protection purchased).

Exhibit 11.1 is a claim scenario that demonstrates how this homeowners' provision might apply to a particular loss. Notice in this particular scenario that the insured receives the ACV. Had the home been 12 years old rather than five, the insured would likely be paid the result of the coinsurance calculation.

Coinsurance Options

The commercial property policy allows the insured the option to use 80%, 90% or 100% coinsurance. As the coinsurance percentage increases, the property rate (or loss cost) decreases. But should 100% coinsurance be used?

From an errors and omissions perspective, probably not. Using 100% coinsurance leaves no room for an incorrect calculation which requires the insured to always have 100 % of the value in force. Even attaching the inflation guard endorsement may not give the insured adequate coverage at the time of the loss.

Insureds that have a commercial property policy also have the opportunity to write all property coverage under a blanket limit of protection. Blanket limit policies are the preferred method when the insured is trying to avoid undervaluing a particular class of property or a particular property location (especially if there are several properties or contents moving among several buildings or locations). However, use of a blanket limit requires the minimum coinsurance percentage be increased to 90%.

One approach CPP insureds can employ to avoid the application of coinsurance is "agreed value." As the name suggests, the agreed value is the value the insured and the underwriter agree the property is worth. Choosing the agreed value option (by indicating this desire on the declarations page) suspends the coinsurance provision for one year. At the end of the year, a new schedule must be submitted and a new agreement reached.

While the agreed value provision is in force, all losses are paid in full up to the limit of coverage, provided the insured purchases coverage equal to the agreed value. If, for some strange reason, the insured does not purchase the agreed value amount, all losses are subject to a form of a coinsurance penalty. But this penalty is based on failure to live up to a separate contract rather than a failure to buy enough coverage.

How Much Coverage

Coinsurance provisions and penalties should not be the deciding factor regarding coverage limits. Forgetting MPL's, PML's and statistical loss chances, the insured should purchase coverage equal to 100% of the property's total insurable value (TIV), based on whether ACV or replacement cost is the valuation method. Buying coverage at this level accomplishes two goals: 1) it avoids the possible application of coinsurance, and 2) it assures that the insured is fully covered for a total loss.

But, as stated above, even though the property is valued at 100% of its TIV, do not increase the commercial client's coinsurance to 100% (even though there is a slight premium break). Use 90% avoid most miscalculation problems and allow some room for an unexpected increase in replacement cost.

Important Coinsurance Conditions and Ideas

- Coinsurance "encourages" insureds to carry relatively high limits of coverage.
- Coinsurance applies to only partial losses. Insureds don't get more than the limits purchased.
- Coinsurance is calculated based on the values at the time of the loss.
- The simplified coinsurance formula is: (Did/Should) x Loss – Deductible = Payment.
- Commercial property policies and homeowners' policies differ on the application of coinsurance.
- Purchase blanket limits of protection when possible (the coinsurance requirement is increased to 90%).

- Use agreed value (remember, the coinsurance requirement is waived, but the insured must purchase the agreed amount).
- Insure at 100% ITV, but don't use 100% coinsurance.

Homeowners' Coinsurance Calculation Examples

Exhibit 11.1

Insured Property Information

Total Insurable Value (TIV): $300,000
Coinsurance Required: 80%
Deductible: $500
Amount of Loss: $50,000
Age of Home: 5 years
Estimated Useful Life: 40 years

Inadequate Limits of Coverage

Amount of Insurance Carried – "Did"	$180,000
Amount of Insurance Required (TIV x Coinsurance) – "Should" ($300,000 x 80%)	$240,000
Coinsurance Penalty Calculation Factors 1. Did/Should ($180,000/$240,000) 2. Loss Amount 3. Deductible	1. 0.75 2. $50,000 3. 500
Coinsurance Penalty Calculation: (1. X 2.) – 3.	(0.75 x $50k) - $500
Amount of Payment (From Coinsurance Penalty Calculation Above)	$37,000
Actual Cash Value of the Loss Factors 1. Age of Home 2. Useful Life 3. Loss 4. Deductible	1. 5 years 2. 40 years 3. $50,000 4. $500
ACV Loss Settlement Calculation: ((2.-1.)/2.)x3.-4.	(35/40) x $50k -$500
Actual Cash Value of the Loss	$43,250
Final Payment Amount	$43,250

In the above scenario, the ACV of the loss is higher than the result of the coinsurance calculation, thus the insured receives the $43,250 ACV. The homeowners' policy states that the insured gets the GREATER of the ACV of the loss or the coinsurance calculation. Obviously the estimated useful life is solely for example purposes. Each situation will vary as the definition of ACV is replacement cost at the time of the loss less physical depreciation. Based on use and environment, some houses depreciate faster than others. Assume the house in this example is 12 years old, the ACV of the loss would be $35,500, meaning that the insured would be paid the coinsurance calculation-producing $37,000.

Chapter 12

How to Calculate the Amount Payable for a Homeowners' Property Loss

Calculating a homeowners' property loss payment seems rather basic – on the surface. But there are a lot of moving parts to consider and apply before arriving at the final payment amount. Exhibit 12.1 is an attempt at walking through the homeowners' property loss payment process. Below are the instructions for its completion. The second page of the flowchart numbers the boxes as described in the instructions below.

The next few paragraphs describe the calculation process as it relates to homeowners' policy property losses in general with a specific focus on the HO-3 with the HO 04 90 endorsement (Personal Property Replacement Cost). These are the key factors initially needed to complete this process.

- Total Damage Amounts to both the dwelling and personal property
- Policy Limits
- Deductible

Total Damage Amount

How much will it actually cost to repair or replace the damaged or destroyed dwelling or personal property? Without this information no other steps can be taken. The "total damage amount" is taken from the proof of loss form supplied to the insured by the insurance carrier after a loss occurs – as detailed in the "Duties After Loss" of the Section I Conditions.

Once the insurance carrier provides and requests the proof of loss form, the insured has 60 days to file the requested information. Notice that the policy does **not** state that the proof is due 60 days from the date of loss; it is due 60 days after requested by the carrier.

The total damage amount obviously can exceed the policy limits. In the flowchart, the policy limits are requested in block "1" for two reasons: 1) later in the process it is needed to calculate any coinsurance penalty that may apply to the dwelling (Coverage "A"), and 2) because the ultimate payout **cannot exceed** the policy limits. **Do not** lower the actual "total damage amount" to match the policy limits as the insured will be penalized when the deductible is subtracted.

Special Limits on Personal Property

Some articles of **personal property** insured by the homeowners' policy are subject to specific sub-limits. Included among this list of limited property are money, securities, watercraft, trailers and personal property used in business. Other property is limited based on the type of loss. For example, jewelry and firearms are limited only if the loss is caused by theft.

In addition to the list of personal property subject to sub-limits, there is a schedule of excluded personal property.

Property insured elsewhere (such as on a personal articles floater), animals, most "motor vehicles," aircraft and property of roomers and boarders is included on this list of excluded property.

A review of the applicable homeowners' policy will provide a full list of both limited personal property and excluded personal property. Box "2" and box "3" in the flowchart apply to both classes of personal property. If there is damaged property subject to a sublimit or excluded entirely, as questioned in box "2," the list of excluded or limited value property is listed in box "3."

Three pieces of information are necessary to complete box "3": 1) a description of the property, 2) the value of that property, and 3) the amount of coverage **allowed** in the policy. All damaged personal property subject to a sublimit is listed on the form. The replacement cost (or ACV depending on the endorsements attached) value of the specified property is listed in the second column labeled "Value." The amount of coverage provided by the policy for that class of property is listed in the third column shown as "Amount Available." If the "Value" is less than the "Amount Available," schedule the actual value. Specifically excluded personal property can also be listed in this box; however, "nothing" or "$0" should be placed in the "Amount Available" column.

The "value" and the "amount available" are totaled and recorded in the last line of the box beside "TOTAL." These amounts are used to develop the insurable "Amount of Personal Property Coverage" detailed in the box "4."

If the personal property "total damage amount" does not include any limited or excluded personal property, boxes "3" and "4" can be skipped and the entire personal property damage amount can be transferred to box "5" (labeled "Actual Insurable Damage).

Calculating the Amount of Personal Property Coverage Available

The full value of limited and excluded personal property (detailed above) must be subtracted from the personal property "total damage amount" (listed in box "1"). The allowable amount of coverage (per the insurance policy as calculated in box "3" is added back to the result. The result is the total "Amount of Personal Property Coverage" indicated at the bottom of box "4."

This total is transferred to the "Personal Property" line found in box "5" labeled "Actual Insurable Damage." As stated in the box, this is the lesser of the "total damage amount" or the product of the calculation detailed above and demonstrated in box "4."

Actual Insurable Damage

At this point in the flowchart, dwelling and personal property limits remain separate as the dwelling coverage must still pass the coinsurance test. The dwelling coverage in box "5" is simply carried forward from the "total damage amount" block. Personal property coverage amounts are the lesser of the amount in box "1" or the "amount of personal property coverage" developed in the fourth block as detailed above.

Coinsurance

Notice that in homeowners' policy the only property subject to a coinsurance calculation is real property. This is explained in greater detail in chapters 10 and 11. Not applying the coinsurance condition to personal property is appropriate since the insured does not necessarily have the opportunity to choose the personal property limit because the amount of coverage is granted as a percentage of the dwelling coverage.

Coinsurance is a function of the amount of insurance carried (IC) compared to the amount of insurance required (IR) by the homeowners' policy coinsurance condition. To be fully insured for **partial real-property losses** the insured must carry 80% of the dwelling's total insurable value **(TIV) at the time of the loss**. (Of course this leaves a gap if there is a loss that exceeds this limit.) Deciphering the insured's compliance with the coinsurance provision is accomplished in boxes "6" and "7."

The basic coinsurance formula (ignoring the deductible) is:

(Insurance Carried (IC)/Insurance Required (IR)) x Loss = Amount Eligible for Payment

Insurance Required (IR) is calculated by multiplying the TIV at the time of the loss by the coinsurance requirement. The coinsurance requirement in the standard homeowners' policy is 80%. To develop "IR" in the standard homeowners' policy, the formula is: TIV x 80% = IR

Insurance Required (IR) is calculated in box "6." If the dwelling policy limit, as scheduled in box "1," is greater than the IR, the coinsurance condition is met and no other calculation is required. Simply add the amount of dwelling damage to the amount of personal property damage listed in the "Actual Insurable Damage" box (box "5") and place that total in the "Total Amount of Insurable Damage" box (box "8").

However, if the policy limit is less than the calculated IR, then the coinsurance condition has not been met and box "7" must be used. This box applies the basic coinsurance formula as presented above to arrive at the "coinsured" value. But, as detailed in the coinsurance series, the homeowners' policy does not apply coinsurance as a penalty. The amount developed applying the coinsurance condition is compared to the dwelling's actual cash value (ACV). The insured is granted the greater of these two values. Essentially, the coinsurance amount is the least the insured will ever get paid in a homeowners' policy subject only to the policy limits.

When a coinsurance calculation is necessary, the result is compared to the dwelling's ACV. The greater of these two values is added to the personal property's actual insurable damage as shown in box "5." This sum is placed in box "8" titled "Total Amount of Insurable Damage." This is the first time the differing values meet.

Deductibles

Deductibles are subtracted from the total amount of insurable loss in property policies. Many make the mistake of trying to subtract the deductible from the policy limit in the event of a total loss. Also, only one deductible applies to a loss. There is not a dwelling deductible and a personal property deductible.

In the flowchart, the deductible (as listed in box "9") is subtracted from the "total amount of insurable damage" to produce the "Amount of Eligible Loss" (found in box "10").

Amount of Eligible Loss

After the application of the deductible to the "total amount of insurable damage," the "amount of eligible loss" is produced and recorded in box "10." This amount is compared to the policy limits. If the policy limits are greater than this amount, the entire amount is paid. If, however, this amount exceeds the policy limits, the insurance is limited to the amount of coverage purchased (the policy limits).

Notice the phrase, "Remember to add all applicable 'Additional Coverages' to this amount" in box "10." The homeowners' policy offers several coverages in addition to the limits purchased. Those amounts must be added to and paid in addition to the "amount of eligible loss."

Examples of these additional coverages include debris removal, reasonable repairs, ordinance or law, loss assessment and fire department service charges. A complete list of additional coverages, their amount and their conditions is found in the homeowners' policy.

Following

Calculating loss payments for commercial property policies is the subject of Chapter 13. While many of these same provisions apply, the differences in the forms require a specific and detailed review.

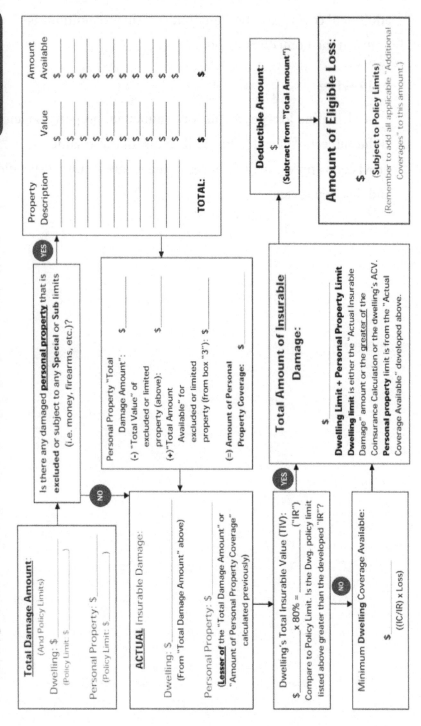

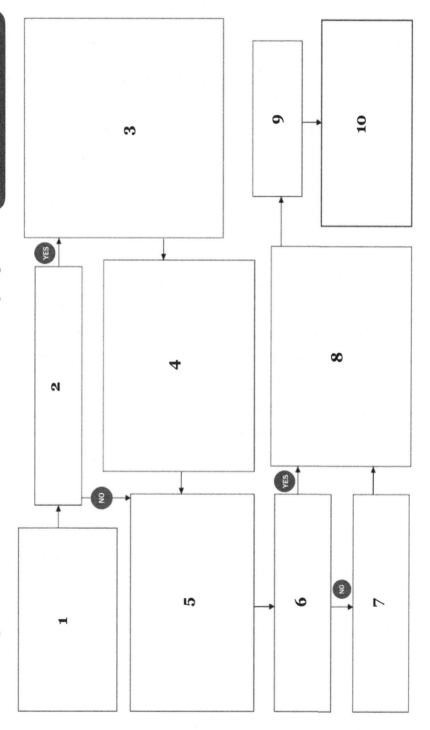

113

Chapter 13

How to Calculate Coverage for a Commercial Property Loss

Working through a commercial property loss closely mirrors the process involved in developing the loss payment for a homeowners' property loss. However, the number of steps required to calculate a commercial property loss is double the number necessary for a homeowners' claim. One of the main reasons for the additional steps is coinsurance. Exhibit 13.1 is the flowchart detailing the CPP loss payment calculation.

Coinsurance applies to both the building coverage and the contents coverage following a commercial property loss. Nearly 75% of the steps in the commercial property loss payment calculation flowchart relate to coinsurance.

A detailed explanation and comparison of the differences between the application of coinsurance in the homeowners' and commercial property policy was provided in chapters 10 and 11. The discussion of coinsurance in this chapter focuses on how to use the information in the flowchart to calculate the amount of the loss that is payable.

Before the payment calculation process can begin, six specific pieces of information are required.

- Total damage amount for both or either the building and contents
- Applicable policy limits for each type of coverage
- Coinsurance percentage
- Deductibles that apply
- Whether the specific property is insured on a replacement cost or actual cash value (ACV) basis
- The value of the covered property, at whichever valuation method is employed, at the time of the loss

Most of this information can be pre-filled before the calculation process begins. Policy limits, the coinsurance percentages, deductibles and how the property is valued can all be filled out before the process begins. But without the amount of damage, nothing can be calculated. Below are the instructions for completing the attached commercial property payment flowchart.

Total Damage Amount

Following a loss, the insurance carrier supplies the insured with a proof of loss form. The proof of loss provides the insurance carrier the specifics surrounding the loss plus a detailed analysis of the amount of loss being claimed – the total damage amount. Once the proof of loss is filed with the carrier, the total damage amount can be transferred to the flowchart and the calculation can then be completed in a matter of minutes.

Both the commercial property policy (CPP) and the homeowners' policy allow the insured 60 days following the insurance carrier's request to complete the proof of loss. Generally, the request for this information is considered made when the carrier provides the insured with the proof of loss form.

Notice once again that the policy does not state that the proof is due 60 days from the date of loss; it is due 60 days after requested.

Obviously, the total damage amount can exceed the policy limits. In the flowchart, the policy limits are requested in box "1" for two reasons: 1) to later calculate any coinsurance penalty that may apply, and 2) because the ultimate payout **cannot exceed** the policy limits. **Do not** lower the "total damage amount" to match the policy limits as the insured will be penalized when the deductible is ultimately subtracted.

Excluded Property

Insurance Services Office's (ISO's) commercial property policy specifically lists 17 types of property excluded from protection (AAIS and proprietary forms may differ). Endorsements are available to add back coverage for some property on this list; some of the scheduled property is completely excluded, but then coverage is given back in small amounts as an "additional coverage;" and some of the excluded property is simply excluded with essentially no standard way to get coverage back.

If any of this excluded property is included in the total damage amount reported on the proof of loss, the value must be deducted from the insurance loss value to arrive at the actual insurable damages. Box "3" is used to schedule the specific property, classify it as building (B) or contents (C) and subtract the value from the total damage amount. The result is the actual insurable damages.

As noted in box "2," if: 1) none of the excluded property is on the proof of loss, or 2) coverage for an otherwise excluded type of property is given back by endorsement, the user can completely skip the deduction process in box "3."

Coinsurance Calculation

Most of this chapter's remaining paragraphs focus on the coinsurance function and its part in calculating the total amount of eligible payment. This section of the discussion is broken into three parts: 1) Developing the "Insurance Required" ("IR"), 2) comparing the "Insurance Carried" ("IC") with the "IR" (the classic coinsurance calculation), and 3) Applying the coinsurance penalty.

Developing the "Insurance Required" ("IR")

Valuation method, the building's or contents' value at the time of loss, and the applicable coinsurance percentage are needed to develop the "insurance required." Lacking any part of this information will not allow the coinsurance calculation to be correctly completed. Inability to correctly complete the coinsurance calculation impedes the ability to correctly establish the amount payable.

The valuation method and the value at the time of the loss are fully linked. Without knowing the valuation method, there is no way to estimate the value of the building or contents. If the proof of loss is completed using replacement cost when the policy provides coverage at actual cash value, the "IR" and entire coinsurance calculation will be inappropriately skewed (potentially resulting in the undue application of a penalty). Having and applying the correct valuation method and value are paramount for the rest of the calculation.

Not only is the valuation method critical, the time at which the property is valued is just as important. When calculating the "insurance required," the damaged property is valued as of the **date of the loss**; not when the original policy was written, the inception date of the policy or any other date – only the date of loss.

Notice that the "IR" is developed separately for the building and contents; this is because one could be replacement cost while the other is ACV. Also, since separate limits are chosen, one class of property could fully meet the coinsurance requirements while the other falls short.

"Insurance required" (the "should" amount) is actually the product of a two-step process. Boxes "5" through "10" walk the completer through the "insurance required" calculation process to aide in the overall coinsurance calculation process.

The building "IR" is found in box "7." Box "10" contains the contents "IR." Box "11" provides the coinsurance calculation comparative (found at the bottom of the first and top of the second page in the flowchart). Information from box "7" is placed in the space labeled, "Building Cov. Required (IR);" The amount developed in box "10" is placed next to, "Contents Cov. Required (IR)" found in box "11."

Comparing Insurance Carried with Insurance Required

Insurance Carried (IC) represents the policy limits the insured actually purchased. In the flowchart, the IC is requested/provided in box "1" (below the amount of damage claimed). Simply place the amount of coverage carried in their respective spots in box "11."

Having IC and IR together in box "11" makes answering the questions found in box "12" and "16" rather simple. Box "12" to the top right of box "11" asks if the building's IC is greater than its IR and box "16" found below box "11" asks the same question, but related instead to contents coverage. The answer to both questions leads the completer through the rest of the coinsurance-related section found in boxes "13" – "15" and "17" – "19."

Applying Coinsurance

Unlike the homeowners' policy, the CPP applies coinsurance as a **penalty**. If the insured does not carry enough coverage, the most it will ever be paid is the result of the coinsurance formula: IC/IR x Loss

As indicated in boxes "13" – "15," if the insured does not carry more than the insurance required (IR), it gets the lesser of the actual damages or the result of the coinsurance calculation. The same penalty applies to the contents coinsurance calculation provided in boxes "17" – "19."

Combined Total Amount of Insurable Damages

All the necessary coinsurance steps are now complete. The total amount of insurable coverage resulting from the comparison and any applicable penalty for both the building and contents damage can be added together to provide the "combined total amount of insurable damages" presented in box "20." This is the first point at which the amount of insurable building damage and insurable contents damage merge.

From here, only one step remains – the application of the deductible. Once the deductible is subtracted, the "amount of eligible loss" is finally calculated.

Deductible

Property deductibles are subtracted from the amount of eligible loss, not the coverage limit or necessarily the amount of the original claim. This is why the deductible appears so late in the flowchart.

The CPP states that only one deductible applies to a loss event. However, it also reads:

When the occurrence involves loss to more than one item of Covered Property and separate Limits of Insurance apply, the losses will not be combined in determining application of the Deductible. But the Deductible will be applied only once per occurrence.

Essentially this means that if the insured has a scheduled CPP (one limit for building and a separate limit for contents) with a $1,000 deductible, the policy will subtract the deductible from the amount of insurable damage that will result in a "penalty."

Assume for example's sake that the building limit ("IC") is $100,000 and the contents "IC" is $50,000. After completing the worksheet, the "Total Amount of Insurable Building Damage" is $102,000 and the "Total Amount of Insurable Contents Damage" is $49,000. What this policy provision means is that the $1,000 deductible will be subtracted from the contents loss and the building damage is subject to the policy limit; this results in a total loss payment of $148,000. Without this provision, the payment would be the full loss amount of $149,000.

This step is not represented in the flowchart. The completer must remember to subtract the deductible from the amount that penalizes the insured the greatest. A note is provided in the flowchart as a reminder.

Obviously, this only applies when there is a total loss and the coinsurance penalty does not apply. Also, this step is only necessary when there are scheduled building and contents limits; blanket limits are not subject to this provision.

Amount of Eligible Loss

After the application of the deductible to the "combined total amount of insurable damage" (subject to the deductible penalty described above) the "amount of eligible loss" is produced and inserted in box "22." The total is compared to the policy limits to assure compliance with the policy language. If the policy limits are greater than this amount, the entire amount is paid. If, however, this amount exceeds the policy limits, the insurance is limited to the amount of coverage purchased (the policy limits).

Again, notice the phrase, "Remember to add all applicable 'Additional Coverages' to this amount." Several additional coverages in addition to the limits are found in the CPP. Those amounts are added to and paid in addition to the "amount of eligible loss."

Examples of additional coverages include debris removal, reasonable repairs, increased cost of construction, fire department service charge and pollutant clean-up and removal. A complete list of additional coverages and coverage extensions, along with each of their amounts and conditions, is found in the CPP.

Calculating Amount Available to Cover a Commercial Property Loss

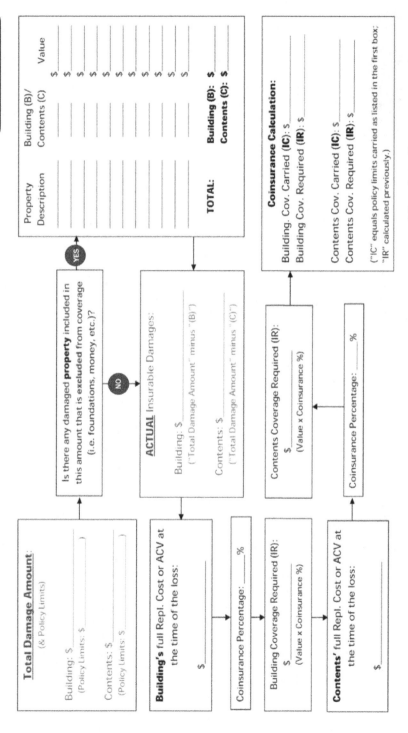

Exhibit 13.1

(Continued on next page)

Calculating Amount Available to Cover a Commercial Property Loss

Exhibit 13.1

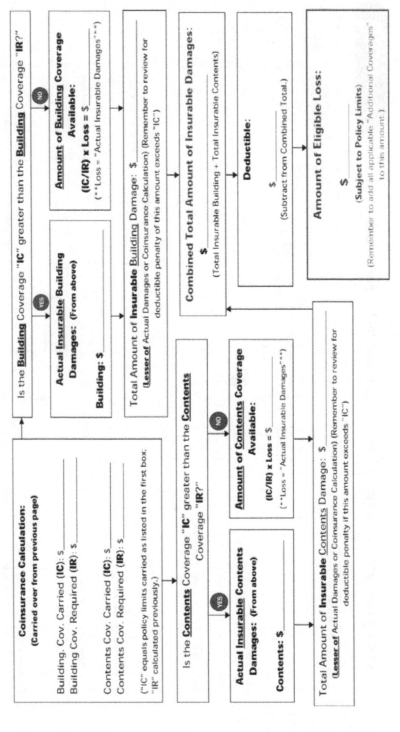

Calculating Amount Available to Cover a Commercial Property Loss

13.1 Numerical Flowcart

(Continued on next page)

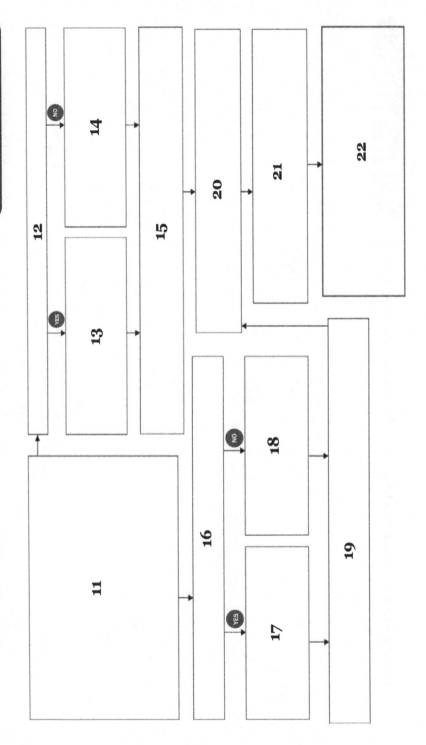

Calculating Amount Available to Cover a Commercial Property Loss

13.1 Numerical Flowcart

Chapter 14

How to Calculate Liability Loss Payments

Calculating liability limits may be a little more straight forward and a bit less process-driven than working through a property loss. Often the slow parts of the process are establishing liability and the amount of actual or claimed liability. But once both are established, the process is rather easy.

Exhibit 14.1 is a liability loss payment flowchart that can be used to walk through the payment calculation process. This flowchart can be used with nearly any liability policy, even umbrella/excess policies. One limitation of this flowchart is split limit auto policies; when a split-limit policy is encountered, simply complete two charts – one for the bodily injury and the second for the property damage.

Although two forms are required when there is a split limit policy, the flowchart actually serves to highlight the application of the bodily injury limits (and by default the property damage limits) for the insured. Since the first value is a sublimit of the second value (i.e. $100,000 per person is a sublimit of $300,000 per accident), the $300,000 can be placed in box "4" because it is, in a sense, an aggregate limit.

Type of Loss (Box 1)

Box "1" requires the user to list the type of liability loss being calculated. Providing this information triggers the user to review the specific policy to discover the limits applying to the particular claim. For instance, if the claim is a fire legal liability claim (more formally known as "Damage to Premises Rented to You") within a commercial general liability (CGL) policy, the completer knows to look in the "Limits of Coverage" section of CGL to locate the coverage limit for this type of loss (which aides in answering the question in the second box).

Be specific when listing the type of loss. Is it a premises/operations property damage claim or a products bodily injury loss? Again, this will key you in to the limits available.

Limits of Coverage (Box 2)

Liability losses are subject to specific limits. Box "1" describing the loss/claim leads the user to the correct limits; the "per-occurrence" or "per-person" limit is entered in box "2." Aggregate limits are not considered at this point.

Aggregate Limits (Boxes 3 and 4) and the Limit Available to Cover the Claim (Box 5)

Once the per-occurrence limit is entered, the next question relates to aggregate limits. An aggregate limit is the maximum the insurance carrier will pay out for a particular type of loss during the policy period. Aggregate limits are reduced by losses paid during the specified period and can even drop below the per occurrence limit provided by the policy (endorsements can be attached to alter this provision).

For example, the insured may have a directors' and officers' policy with limits of $1 million per act and $2 million aggregate. If that insured experiences three losses totaling $1.5 million, there is only $500,000 remaining in the aggregate account. Thus, the amount available to pay any future losses is limited by the aggregate.

Box "3" asks if an aggregate limit applies to the specific loss. If yes, the aggregate REMAINING amount is listed in box "4." If there is no aggregate, box "4" is skipped and the per-occurrence limit is inserted in box "5."

In the case of split limit auto policies, the per-accident limit is listed in box "4" (as stated above). Since each person will lower the "per accident" limit, a separate flowchart will need to be completed for each injured person indicating the reduction of the per accident limit by each injured person. In addition, a separate property damage chart must be completed. (Remember, these multiple charts are only required in split limit situations or when multiple limits apply to a loss.)

The per-occurrence limit is compared to the remaining aggregate limit. The **lesser of** the two amounts is entered as the "Limit Available to Cover the Claim" in box "5."

Amount of Loss or Damage Claimed (Box 6)

At this point, liability has been established. Box "6" is where the amount of loss or damage claimed by the third party is entered. Court rulings, medical bills, damage estimates, claims by the injured party or settlements are all examples of sources for this information. Once the amount of the damage for which the insured is responsible (liable for) is known, the amount is entered in box "6."

Self-Insured Retention (Box 7)

Self-insured retentions are the responsibility of the insured regardless of the amount of the claim. Unlike a property deductible, which can disappear if the total loss exceeds the policy limit, a self-insured retention essentially acts like the first layer of coverage.

In this flowchart, the SIR is deducted from only the amount of loss or damage claimed by the injured third party recorded in box "6" not the limit available to cover the claim reported in box "5." Two absolutely interconnected reasons for the placement of the SIR deduction in this flowchart are:

1. The SIR is the first layer of **coverage**, thus the amount claimed could be higher than the policy limit yet still be fully covered because....
2. The maximum the insurer is going to pay is the policy limits in **addition** to the SIR.

As an example, assume that the amount of coverage available to pay a particular claim is $100,000, the SIR is $10,000 and the amount of injury claimed by the third party is $105,000. The claim is higher than the policy limit, but once the $10,000 SIR is deducted, the maximum possible claim is

$95,000 – fully within the policy limit. In this example, any claim $110,000 or less is fully covered by the combination of the insured (as the first $10,000 layer) and the insurer (as the second $100,000 layer).

Likewise, if the claim made by the third party is only $60,000 the first $10,000 is paid by the insured as the SIR and the remaining $50,000 is paid by the insurer. The SIR is nearly always the first layer of protection (unless the policy wording provided otherwise as in some executive and professional liability forms).

Maximum Possible Claim (Box 8)

As detailed in the SIR section, the "maximum possible claim" is the amount claimed by the injured party minus the applicable SIR. The developed amount is compared to the policy limit (again, recorded in box "5") to determine the amount paid by the insurance carrier.

Amount Paid by Insurer (Box 9)

The **maximum** the policy is going to pay is the lesser of the "limit available to cover the claim" (found in box "5") and the "maximum possible claim" (developed in box "8"). The lower of these two values is placed in box "9" representing the amount the insurer is expected to pay for the subject liability claim. As noted in the box, if the policy provides any supplementary or additional coverage, remember to add them to this amount as they are paid in addition to the policy limit.

Notice that there are two boxes remaining in the flowchart. These calculate the claim amount that must be paid as either out-of-pocket expense or passed to an umbrella or excess liability policy.

Adequate Limits (Boxes 10 and 11)

Boxes "10" and "11" do not play a part in calculating the amount of claims payment made by the insured. All the information necessary to complete the payment calculation is provided in boxes "1" through "9." Only the question of coverage adequacy is handled in boxes "10" and "11." Box "10" asks the key question, is the amount of coverage available (reported in box "5") equal to or greater than the "maximum possible claim" (as indicated in box "8")?

If the answer is "no," the difference between the maximum possible claim and the amount of coverage available is entered in box "11." If there is an umbrella or excess policy available, the amount in this box should be carried over to the flowchart for that policy. However, if there is no umbrella or excess policy, this represents the out-of-pocket amount the insured will be called upon to pay.

How to Calculate the Amount of Liability Coverage Available

Exhibit 14.1

Type of Liability Loss (GL, Auto, Professional, Executive, Umbrella, etc.):

_____

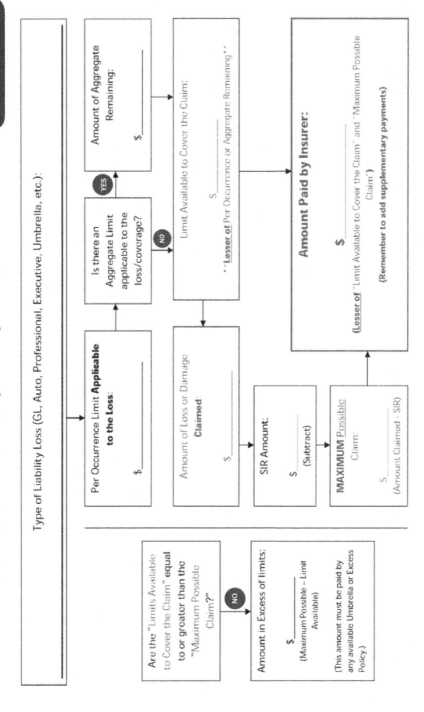

Per Occurrence Limit **Applicable to the Loss**:

$ _____

Is there an Aggregate Limit applicable to the loss/coverage?

YES → Amount of Aggregate Remaining:

$ _____

NO

Limit Available to Cover the Claim:

$ _____

Lesser of Per Occurrence or Aggregate Remaining**

Amount of Loss or Damage Claimed:

$ _____

SIR Amount:

$ _____ (Subtract)

MAXIMUM Possible Claim:

$ _____ (Amount Claimed - SIR)

Are the "Limits Available to Cover the Claim" equal to or greater than the "Maximum Possible Claim?"

NO

Amount in Excess of limits:

$ _____ (Maximum Possible – Limit Available)

(This amount must be paid by any available Umbrella or Excess Policy.)

Amount Paid by Insurer:

$ _____

(**Lesser of** "Limit Available to Cover the Claim" and "Maximum Possible Claim")

(Remember to add supplementary payments)

How to Calculate the Amount of Liability Coverage Available

14.1 Numerical Flowcart

Chapter 15

'Occurrence' vs. 'Claims Made' Liability Coverage Forms

One of two coverage "trigger" forms is used to provide liability protection: the "occurrence form" or the "claims made" form. There is no difference in the breadth of coverage provided by either form, the difference lies in what "triggers" the policy to respond – the occurrence of injury or damage or a claim (as defined by the policy) arising out of the injury or damage.

Agents and insureds are likely more familiar with the occurrence version of the form. Until the mid-60's the "claims made" wording didn't exist; and even into the early-to-mid 70's its use was sporadic. Today the occurrence form remains the dominant form except for most professional and executive liability exposures where "claims made" policies rule. On occasion, a "claims made" form may be found insuring an unusual risk or "high" risk class of business (its use is more common in "non-standard" policies).

"Occurrence," "Occurrence" Forms & Legal Theories

The term "occurrence" relates to the injury itself. When did the injury "occur?" Once the date of "occurrence" is established, insureds know which policy responds to the incident. Simply put, the policy in effect when the injury "occurs" defends and/or pays the loss.

However, there is no one legal theory used to determine the date(s) of an "occurrence." Courts apply four legal theories to identify when bodily injury or property damage occurs. Additionally, each jurisdiction looks to its own case law and legal precedent to decide which of these theories pertain to a particular incident.

1. The "**Injury-in-Fact Theory**": Courts subscribing to this theory consider the date of ANY ACTUAL injury/damage (the day the nail was driven into the electrical wire) as the date of the "occurrence," regardless of the discovery or manifestation of the injury.

2. The "**Manifestation Theory**": The date the injury becomes EVIDENT is the date of the "occurrence" (i.e. the day the fire starts because of the nail in the wire). This theory is applied by the majority of states.

3. The "**Exposure Theory**": Courts consider the dates of exposure to be the dates of the "occurrence" (multiple policy potential).

4. The "**Continuous Trigger Theory**": This is also known as the "triple-trigger" theory. Multiple occurrence dates (and thus multiple policies) may be involved based on: the date of first exposure, the dates of continuous exposure, and the dates of manifestation.

(The "Exposure Theory" and the "Continuous Trigger Theory" generally apply to pollution and like claims with longer exposure and manifestation periods. Asbestos and similar injuries and claims are examples of the use of these injury theories.)

Several occurrence-based policies might be called upon to respond to one claim of bodily injury or property damage – depending on which legal theory is applied. Claims of injuries involving long "gestation" periods (long time lapses between the initial act or error and the ultimate result) are likely to span several policy periods. Injuries resulting from any professional malpractice and pollution injuries are two prime examples.

In an effort to eliminate the uncertainty of which (and how many) policies will be involved and pulled into these "long-tail" losses, the insurance industry introduced the "claims made" policy. With a "claims made" form, coverage is triggered by the claim itself. Again, simply stated, the policy in effect when the claim is brought, defends and/or pays the loss.

"Claims Made" Differences

Unlike an occurrence-based policy, where only the date of occurrence must be determined (or occurrences – based on the legal theory applied), three dates must be known and/or determined to trigger coverage in a "claims made" form.

1. The Date of Occurrence
2. The Retroactive Date (or prior and pending litigation date)

3.   The Date the "Claim" is Made

The date of occurrence has already been discussed and the date the claim is made might be considered self-evident (even though there is some doubt about what constitutes a "claim" and when it is made); thus only the term "retroactive date" necessitates further explanation.

A retroactive date acts as a limiting provision in the "claims made" policy. If the injury or damage occurs **BEFORE** this date – the policy will not respond to the loss. If, however, the covered injury or damage occurs **AFTER** the retroactive date, the policy in effect when the claim is made will respond to defend and/or pay the claim.

For example, a policy has a January 1, 2004, retroactive date and the injury is determined to have occurred on November 1, 2003. The claim (as defined by the policy) arising from the occurrence is made on February 1, 2004. In this example, the policy in effect on February 1, 2004, **will NOT** pay for or defend the injury because the occurrence/injury took place before the retroactive date. Worse, the prior policy may not pay the loss if it was also a "claims made" policy whose retroactive date was advanced at renewal (either by the expiring carrier or due to a change in carriers).

Continuing the above simplified example, if the retroactive date were January 1, 2003, the policy in effect on February 1, 2004, (when the claim is made) would respond in defense or payment of the injury. Both examples are overly simplified, but they should make clear the importance of the retroactive date and its effect on coverage availability.

Moving Between Occurrence and Claims Made Liability Forms

Insureds may find themselves in the position of having to move from one liability coverage trigger form to another. Either from an "occurrence" form to a "claims made" form, or vice versa. One move has the possibility of a coverage gap, the other results in an absolute coverage gap. But most gaps can be filled.

Moving from an "occurrence" to a "claims made" form creates little chance for a coverage gap – based, of course, on which legal theory of "occurrence" is used and the nature of the insured's operations. However, going from a 'claims made' to an 'occurrence' policy almost always leaves a gap in protection.

"Occurrence" to "Claims Made"

Keep in mind, if the insured is covered by an "occurrence" form, the policy in effect when the injury or damage **occurs** pays the claim. As long as the injury or damage occurs during the policy period, the policy responds – regardless of when the claim is brought (subject to statutes of limitation and repose).

Insureds whose actions result in immediate or nearly immediate injury or manifestation of injury will likely experience no coverage gap. However, insureds whose actions may not manifest in injury for a long period of time may experience a gap in protection if the injury, according to the court, does not legally "occur" until some point after the "occurrence" form has expired.

Two possible options for closing this coverage gap are: 1) the insured can purchase a "discontinued operations" endorsement (it's like tail coverage for an "occurrence" form), or 2) get agreement from the "claims made" carrier to provide full prior acts coverage (no retro date). The second is obviously the preferred option. If the application contains a warranty provision and the insurer does not feel it is picking up any undue exposures, the second option should be relatively easy to accomplish (in theory). If nothing else, get the underwriter to move the retro date back three or five years if possible.

(There are other uses for the discontinued operations coverage, but those are outside the scope of this chapter. The key to remember about the importance of discontinued operations coverage is that the policy only pays for claims that "occur" during the policy period. If the insured goes out of business or sells to another and cancels or non-renews coverage; they may have no coverage if "injury" or "damage" "occurs" at some point after the policy has ended.)

"Claims Made" to "Occurrence"

With a "claims made" form, three dates must be satisfied, the occurrence date, the policy effective date and the retroactive date. As long as the injury occurs after the retro date, the policy in effect when the **claim** is brought (not when the injury occurs) defends/pays the claim.

Insureds going from a "claims made" to an "occurrence" form have a gap in liability protection. If the injury occurs during the claims made policy but the claim doesn't arrive until after policy expiration, there is no coverage provided by either policy. Why? Because the occurrence form, as stated above, only pays if the injury occurs during **its** policy period and the claims made form only pays if the **claim** is made during the policy period. The example loss meets neither of these requirements because the injury occurred before the "occurrence" form existed and the claim came after the "claims made" form expired – thus such loss is not covered.

The only way to avoid this gap is to purchase a supplemental extended reporting period (SERP) (aka a "tail") endorsement before switching over to the "occurrence" form. The SERP, in simplified terms, allows the insured up to a specified amount of time following policy expiration to report a claim for any injury that "occurred" during the expired policy period and after any specified retroactive date (or prior and pending litigation date). The SERP states that it will treat such claims as if they were filed on the last day of the "claims made" policy. Some SERP's reinstate the aggregate limits and some do not; a review of the form is required.

Short of a SERP, the insured has no usual and customary way to fill the gap created when moving from a "claims made" to an "occurrence" form. Some "occurrence" form carriers have agreed to provide "nose-" type coverage as a manuscripted endorsement onto the "occurrence" form. This is akin to prior acts coverage in the "claims made" form. The incidents of this endorsement's use are rare and probably cannot be counted on to fill this gap. SERP's may remain the only option.

Chapter 16

How to Prepare for and Evaluate the Consent to Settle and the 'Hammer Clause'

Generally found in professional liability, errors and omissions and executive liability coverage forms, insurance industry practitioners affectionately refer to the entire consent to settle clause as the "hammer clause." Mostly because one small part acts to "hammer" the insured into compliance with the insurance carrier's desire to settle a claim.

This is a mischaracterization of the entire clause. The consent to settle clause is, of itself, advantageous to the "innocent" (or at least not-liable) insured with only one part of the clause containing a penalty for not consenting. Further, not every consent to settle provision contains a "hammer clause" (most do, but not all).

Which Liability Forms Contain "Consent to Settle" Language

Commercial general liability (CGL) policies grant solely to the insurance carrier the right to settle any claim. The insured cannot oppose or disallow a settlement. The carrier's right to settle is reasonable considering the types of losses covered by the CGL (bodily injury, property damage and personal and advertising injury). Rarely do any of these injuries or damages harm the insured's reputation in the community or industry.

However, some individuals and entities occupy a position of trust arising out of presumed knowledge, training and/or professional or legal guidelines. A perceived or real violation of this trust, even unintentional, can cause a type of loss or injury to a third party not anticipated in or covered by the CGL. Charges made against an insured for violation of this trust, if proved in court or even settled out of court, can damage the insured's reputation and future business. This is because the charges convey a negative connotation regarding the way the insured conducts business or practices its profession.

Insureds subject to this **indirect reputational loss exposure** are generally granted the opportunity to decide if a settlement is appropriate (consent to settle). If the insured does not feel a settlement is warranted, they have the right to refuse the carrier's recommendation to settle, but doing so may subject them to a severe penalty pending the outcome of a trial or judgment depending on the breadth of the "hammer clause" provision contained within the consent to settle wording.

Only a few policy types protect insureds against this violation of trust arising out of charges of poor management or improper professional practices. "Consent to settle" wording is nearly always found in the following policy types.

- ***Professional Liability Policies***: This includes such coverages as medical malpractice, lawyer's professional liability, architect's and engineer's professional liability and pastoral professional liability (not an all-inclusive list). These policies insure the specified professionals in the event they inadvertently misperform their trained-for duties.

- *Errors and Omissions Policies*: The most commonly considered is insurance agent's errors and omissions (E&O) coverage. This coverage is also purchased by mortgage brokers, investment counselors, real estate brokers and other such operations. An E&O policy provides protection against the financial consequences of an incorrectly performed special duty owed to clients or members of the public.

- *Executive Liability Policies*: Directors and officers (D&O), employment practices liability insurance (EPLI) and fiduciary liability insurance are examples of executive liability policies. Each of these, in some way, protect against the financial consequences of mismanagement of the business

Differences between "Professionals" and "Non-Professionals" from an Insurance Perspective

Professional liability and errors and omissions coverage are described separately above to highlight the difference between the individuals or entities covered by the policies. "Professionals," for liability purposes, are generally those that require some level of organized higher education to initially qualify for entry into the field and ultimately full licensure. For example, doctors must complete medical school to be eligible to practice; architects must attain the proper degree to perform architects's duties, as do engineers to perform their duties. Professionals are commonly subject to some type of peer review in the event of a malpractice.

Errors and omissions liability is generally reserved for those whose actions or inactions could result in another person's or entity's unexpected or undeserved financial loss. Individuals protected by E&O policies are generally not required to have a specific amount or focus of education. A license to work in one of these areas may be required by a particular governing jurisdiction (state or federal government), but beyond that, there are few barriers to entry. Rarely are operations that qualify for E&O coverage subject to regulatory investigation.

Why Consent to Settle Language is Necessary

Reputation and good will, although hard to value, are of utmost importance to a business. A doctor can have the most modern and inviting office in the country, but if he is known to have poor bed-side manner or to be a mediocre medical practitioner, his practice will likely suffer. The same is true of the company that is viewed as discriminatory in its employment practices. Neither will do as well as they could with a better public image. Such entities need the ability to protect their image against harm based on unfounded or trumped-up charges, thus the creation of the consent to settle provision.

A certain amount of tension exists between the insured and the insurance carrier when the consent to settle clause is available. The insurance carrier wants to protect its reputation if it feels there has been no wrong doing, or at least nothing different from the usual and customary practices.

Without the consent to settle language, the insurance carrier could settle the claim regardless of the insured's opinion (just as in the CGL) or really any regard for the insured's reputation. Consent to settle language gives the insured a voice, allowing them to make a business decision regarding the merits of the case, the effects of a settlement and the possible result should the offered settlement be refused. It's the result following a refused settlement around which the "hammer clause" is based.

Application of the "Hammer Clause"

Few words are as dangerous in the insurance contract as "however." Nearly everything prior to it is negated by its presence. The "hammer clause" follows the "however" in the consent to settle provision. The extent of the "however" varies from form to form and carrier to carrier.

A Hammer by any Other Name

The provisions of the "hammer clause" seek to convince the insured to accept the settlement offer by spelling out the consequences if the offer is refused. Other names for the "hammer clause" are the "cooperation clause" and the "coinsurance clause" (not like the coinsurance used in property coverage). Regardless of the term used, the effect is generally the same; the insured is penalized for not accepting the settlement if the total judgment amount plus defense exceeds the amount for which the claim could have been settled.

Different levels of penalty exist among the many hammer clauses ranging from an absolute exclusion of all amounts over settlement to those where the insurance carrier and the insured split the amount over the settlement amount by a pre-determined percentage. The varying degrees are discussed below.

The Bigger the Hammer, the Greater the Damage

Two distinct hammer clauses exist: the "full hammer" (for lack of a better term) and the "modified hammer". The "full hammer" is more common and its penalty is much greater. The "modified hammer" is often referred to as a coinsurance clause.

The "Full Hammer"

Essentially, the "full hammer" states that if the insured refuses to consent to settlement, the most the insurance carrier will pay is the amount for which the claim could have been settled plus the defense cost incurred to that point of the settlement acceptance.

The "Modified Hammer"

Insurers choosing to use the "modified hammer" do not punish the insured as extensively as the carriers applying "full hammer" wording. This is often referred to as the coinsurance clause because the insurance company agrees to split the amount with the insured that exceeds the accepted settlement plus defense costs to that point, essentially making the insured a "coinsurer" on all amounts over the settlement amount.

The two most commonly used "modified hammer" clause coinsurance percentages are 50% and 70%. Each percentage is the amount the insurance carrier will pay, so if 70% is used, the insurer will pay 70% of all amounts over the settlement amount plus defense cost to that point. Of course, the amount paid by the carrier is subject to (and limited by) the limit of liability carried.

A Little Velvet on the Hammer

Some policy wording works to entice the insured to agree to the settlement by offering incentives. The most common being the reduction of any self-insured retention or deductible if the insured accepts the settlement.

Variations of the above-presented "hammer clause" provisions exist. Some are hybrids combining the "full hammer" and "modified hammer" for different expenses (i.e. the "full hammer" applies to defense costs while the "modified hammer" wording applies to the amount of damages paid). These variations and hybrids are not discussed as the above are the most common provisions; plus, understanding the full and modified hammer allows an understanding of any combination of the two.

The "Hammer's" Effect on Coverage Limits

Once the insurance carrier has gained the injured party's acceptance of a settlement amount, the insured's coverage limits are reduced, regardless of the limits purchased. In effect, the insured no longer has access to the full amount of coverage they purchased at policy inception. Of course, the total penalty is based on whether a "full hammer" or "modified hammer" clause is in use.

To demonstrate the effect on limits of each major type of hammer clause, consider the following loss scenario: A female employee sues a large corporation for $2 million alleging sexual harassment. The suit is immediately turned over to the employment practices liability insurance (EPLI) carrier to provide defense and coverage for any judgment (up to policy limits).

During the pre-trial negotiations, the plaintiff agrees to a $500,000 settlement which is immediately communicated to the insured corporation. Because of the consent to settle wording, the insurance carrier cannot simply pay to settle, the insured must give permission.

After conducting its own internal investigation, the corporation is convinced that none of its employees or management did anything inappropriate. The corporation comes to the conclusion that the employee is simply trying to "shake them down." Because of their own findings and fear that a settlement would trigger more people to try to pursue such suits, the corporation refuses the settlement, opting to take the case to court.

At trial and on appeal the corporation loses. The plaintiff is awarded $1,200,000 and defense costs total another $300,000. The total cost of the claim is $1,500,000.

For purposes of this example, the insured has a $2 million per occurrence limit. Two assumptions are made as well: 1) defense costs are within the limits of coverage, and 2) when the settlement offer is accepted, defense costs total $100,000 (the policy will pay $600,000 from the policy limit). Self-insured retentions are ignored in this example. How will each of the "hammer clauses" respond to this non-consent based on the above information?

"Full Hammer" Response: Before commencing trial, the insured knows that the most the insurance carrier is going to pay is $600,000. Why? Because the full hammer clause states that the maximum paid is the amount for which the claim could have been settled plus defense costs incurred up to the day the settlement offer was accepted by the injured party. The insured must pay $900,000 out of its own cash.

A cousin to the "full hammer" is the "**pounding hammer**" (again, for lack of a better term). This takes the hammer clause one step further stating that if the insured refuses to settle and insists on continuing to fight, they do so on their own. The insurance carrier pays to the insured the amount of accepted settlement plus incurred defense costs to the point of acceptance and steps out of the picture. The insured becomes responsible for its own defense (and the associated costs) and any judgment over the amount already paid to the insured. Such a pounding hammer generally convinces the insured to settle. Here is an example of such language.

> *"Our duty to defend also ends if you fail or refuse to consent to a settlement we recommend and the claimant will accept. You must then defend the claim at your own expense. As a consequence of such failure or refusal, our liability for loss shall not exceed the amount for which we could have settled such claim had you consented, plus claim expenses incurred prior to the time we made such recommendation."*

"Modified Hammer" Response: Depending on the coinsurance percentage applied, the "modified hammer" is far less punishing than the full hammer. If the coinsurance percentage is 50%, the insurer pays all of the $600,000 for which they could have settled plus 50% of all amounts over that, in this case $450,000. In total, the insurance carrier pays $1,050,000 and the insured pays $450,000 (again, ignoring SIR's). Had the coinsurance percentage been 70%, the insurer would pay the $600,000 plus $630,000 (70% of the remaining $90,000) for a total of $1,230,000. The insured would be responsible for only $270,000.

Hybrid Hammers

"Modified" and "Full Hammer" hybrids can also be found. The most common divide expenses into two classes: 1) amount to cover the judgment for the wrongful act (loss amount), and 2) defense cost. These hybrid forms often apply the "modified hammer's" coinsurance percentage to the loss amount, but a "full hammer" type wording is used for the defense cost (limiting coverage for defense cost to the amount incurred when the settlement was accepted).

Under this policy wording scenario, the 50% coinsurance policy would pay $950,000 ($500,000 settlement + $100,000 defense + $350,000 of remaining loss amount). The $200,000 additional defense cost incurred after the accepted settlement offer plus the remaining $350,000 loss amount would be the responsibility of the insured. Likewise, a 70% coinsurance form pays $1,090,000, leaving the insured responsible for the remaining $410,000.

Defense costs are not only subject to the consent to settle provision, but also general policy provisions. Some (if not most) policies presented in this chapter include defense costs within the limits of coverage, but a few pay defense in addition to the limit of purchased liability. How the policy responds to defense costs in general will directly affect the way defense costs are handled in the hammer clause.

Hear the Hammer Ring

A "full hammer" may be less expensive than a "modified hammer", but the damage it can cause following a loss makes the "modified hammer", or some hybrid, a far better option. Knowing the purpose of these clauses (and how they apply) strengthen the agent/client relationship.

Chapter 16 – Consent to Settle and the 'Hammer Clause'

Providing insureds the best policy for the premium is the goal, or at least should be, of every agent. Knowing how the competing policies apply the consent to settle and hammer clause is an important consideration when comparing forms.

Chapter 17

Does 2+8+9=1? Understanding Covered Auto Symbols in the Business Auto Policy

Insurance Services Office's (ISO's) Business Auto Coverage (BAC) form protects the named insured (the "you") against the financial consequences of its legal liability for bodily injury or property damage not excluded by the policy and arising out of the ownership, maintenance or use of a "covered auto." This makes the **covered auto symbols** the key to the business auto policy. Each symbol grants insured auto status to a different class of vehicle.

Nine pre-defined coverage symbols (1-9) trigger protection to a progressively narrowing definition of insured vehicles. For example, Symbol "1" extends protection to "Any Auto," while Symbol "7" provides coverage for only "Specifically Described Autos." The ability to add "special instruction" symbols (10,11, etc.) exist beyond the nine specifically defined symbols. A relatively recent edition to the list of covered auto symbols is "19," which extends coverage for "mobile equipment" that, for whatever reason, must be registered for use on public roads.

The agent's goal is (or should be) to use the broadest symbol allowed to extend coverage to the greatest number of vehicle **classes** (owned, hired or borrowed).

This chapter includes copyrighted material of ISO Properties, Inc. with its permission.

Symbol "1" – Any Auto

"Any," as provided in Symbol "1," contains NO limitations. It means exactly what it says. Regardless of the "auto's" status as owned, non-owned, hired, borrowed or whatever, it is covered. The only limitations on "Any Auto" are the policy exclusions. Essentially, if the named insured (the "you") or "automatic insured" (subject to five exceptions) are held legally liable for injury arising out of the ownership, maintenance or non-excluded use of an auto, the BAC provides coverage.

Symbol "1" is almost exclusively a liability coverage symbol. It is unlikely to find it used with any other auto policy coverage type (medical payments, uninsured & underinsured motorist or physical damage).

Due to the breadth of insured vehicle status granted by Symbol "1" (owned, non-owned and hired), it should be used to trigger liability coverage whenever possible. However, use of Symbol "1" may not always be appropriate. Specific inappropriate Symbol "1" usage generally flows from unique risk characteristics of a particular insured.

Equaling Symbol "1"

Beyond the rare cases of inappropriate Symbol "1" usage, there are occasions when underwriters simply will not entertain extending liability protection to "Any Auto." Such refusal might be class-based or simply because the carrier's underwriting philosophy is not to provide Symbol "1."

Accomplishing the goal of providing the broadest definition of insured vehicle without the ability to use Symbol

"1" requires a combination of three covered auto symbols: "2" (Owned Autos Only), "8" (Hired Autos) and "9" (Non-Owned Autos). Using Symbols "2," "8" and "9" appear to cover the full range of insured vehicle definitions, but do they? Does **2+8+9=1?**

Judging the effectiveness of this option's ability to accomplish the goal, each covered auto symbol requires review.

Descriptions of Symbols "2," "8" and "9"

Each symbol definition contains clues as to this combination's ability to meet the breadth of covered vehicle definition offered by Symbol "1." Following are the applicable definitions found in ISO's Business Auto Coverage Form.

- **Symbol "2" (Owned "Autos" Only)**: Only those "autos" you own (and for Liability Coverage and "trailers" you don't own while attached to power units you own). This includes those "autos" you acquire ownership of after the policy begins.
- **Symbol "8" (Hired "Autos" Only):** Only those "autos" you lease, hire, rent or borrow. This does not include any "auto" you lease, hire, rent, or borrow from any of your "employees," partners (if you are a partnership), member (if you are a limited liability company) or members of their households.
- **Symbol "9" (Non-owned "Autos" Only):** Only those "autos" you do not own, lease, hire, rent, or

borrow that are used in connection with your business. This includes "autos" owned by your "employees," partners (if you are a partnership), members (if you are a limited liability company), or members of their households but only while used in your business or your personal affairs. (Note: Essentially, Symbol "9" extends vicarious liability protection to the named insured (the "you") for bodily injury or property damage to a third party caused by someone operating a covered vehicle on the named insured's behalf or for their benefit.)

Two important terms must be considered when comparing the breadth of inclusion offered by the amalgamation of these three symbols compared to Symbol "1": "you" (the named insured) and "covered auto" (as defined by each symbol above).

Why "You" Matters

Liability insurance forms always extend the greatest amount of protection to the policy's "you" (also known as the named insured). The BAC is no exception. The definitions of Symbols "2," "8" and "9" refer to the policy's "you" where Symbol "1" does not. This is the first clue that these two options are not equal in breadth of protection.

Who "you" is differs based on the insured's legal structure as a sole proprietor, partner, limited liability company (LLC) or corporation as follows:

- **Sole proprietor**: The individually named owner is the policy's "you." So the individual must own, hire or borrow the vehicle. For non-owned coverage to apply, the owner of the non-owned vehicle must be doing something to further the proprietor's business.

- **Partnerships:** Like sole proprietors, the partners are the "you" of the policy. Essentially the same provisions apply to partnerships as sole proprietors.

- **Limited liability companies (LLC's):** The LLC is the named insured (subject to some state laws), but the policy treats the members of the LLC the same as partners.

- **Corporations (any type):** The corporation is the "you" in the policy making everyone else an "employee" including the "owner" of the corporation.

These differing assignments of "you" status leads to gaps in coverage when Symbols "2," "8" and "9" are used in place of "1." Symbols "8" and "9" are where the gaps reside.

Symbol "1" – Still the Best

Use of the triune symbol options provide nearly the same breadth of coverage as Symbol "1," but not completely. At least two coverage gaps keep the "Any Auto" option the preferred choice.

Automobile rental. Symbol "8" does not provide coverage to the **named insured** (the "you") or the employee if he rents the car in his personal name rather than the business name. Symbol "1" would provide coverage to the named insured but not the employee. However, both gaps can be filled by the attachment of CA 20 54 (Employee Hired Autos) which extends coverage to employees who lease autos in their personal name.

Borrowing an employee's car. Symbol "8" specifically states that a car "you" (the named insured) borrow from an employee is not a "hired" vehicle. And Symbol "9" only extends vicarious liability protection to the named insured for the employee's use of their personal vehicle on the named insured's account. Coverage gaps are created when the named insured is a sole proprietor, partner and possibly an LLC. Since these individuals are considered the "you" and the definition specifically excludes coverage for any "you" that borrows an "auto" from an employee (etc.), there is no coverage under the BAC for bodily injury or property damage caused by the used of that borrowed "auto." Symbol "1" contains no such exclusions; the insured entity would still be protected by the policy.

Vicarious Liability

Symbol "9" extends a certain level of vicarious liability to the named insured for the actions of the owners of a non-owned auto. But the "degrees of separation" protected by the use of this symbol are not crystal clear.

Protection extended by Symbol "9" is limited to specifically-defined non-owned autos "**used in connection with your business**." There exists no definition in the policy for "**connection**." Does the insured (the "you") have to directly benefit from the use of the vehicle for coverage to apply; or is only a casual, indirect connection required?

Without a clear directive regarding the extent of coverage, this produces a possible third gap between the use of Symbol "1" and the three replacement symbols.

Finish Line

If Symbol "1" is not available for whatever reason, use "2," "8" and "9." The combination does not completely provide the same breadth of protection, but it is very close. Using multiple symbols to provide auto protection can be compared to trying to create an "all risk" policy (a bad term) by lengthening the list of covered named perils. The two will never provide the same breadth of protection.

*(**Ending note**: If Symbol "2" is unavailable, try using Symbols "3," "4," "8" and "9." Symbol "3" is owned private passenger autos and Symbol "4" is owned autos other than private passenger; essentially 3+4=2.)*

The BAC's Remaining Coverage Symbols

As mentioned at the beginning of this chapter, the BAC form specifically defines nine auto symbols. Symbols "1," "2," "8" and "9" were defined and explored above. Following are brief explanations of the remaining coverage symbols.

- **Symbol 3 – Owned Private Passenger "Autos" Only:** As the title suggests, use of this symbol limits protection to only private passenger autos owned by the insured. If the insured acquires any private passenger autos during the policy period, protection is extended to these vehicles during the remainder of the policy period. Use of this symbol is generally limited to liability coverage.

- **Symbol 4 – Owned "Autos" Other Than Private Passenger "Autos" Only:** Like Symbol 3, this symbol extends coverage to owned autos, but this extends coverage to only "other than private passenger autos" such as trucks (light, medium, heavy and extra-heavy). In addition to the vehicle, protection is extended to any non-owned trailer while attached to a vehicle protected under this symbol. If the insured acquires additional "other than private passenger autos" during the policy period, protection is extended to these vehicles during the remainder of the policy period. Use of this symbol is generally limited to liability coverage.

- **Symbol 5 – Owned "Autos" Subject to No-Fault:** This symbol is used when a vehicle is licensed and principally garaged in a state subject to "no-fault" (aka. Personal Injury Protection (PIP)) statutes. Extends coverage to any autos acquired during the policy period. As suggested, this symbol is limited to liability coverage.

- **Symbol 6 – Owned "Autos" Subject to Compulsory Uninsured Motorists Laws:** This symbol is used when a vehicle is licensed and principally garaged in a state subject to uninsured motorist statutes. In these states, the insured cannot reject uninsured motorist coverage. This extends coverage to any autos acquired during the policy period. As suggested, this symbol is limited to uninsured motorist coverage.

- **Symbol 7 – Specifically Described "Autos":** Use of this symbol limits coverage only to those autos specifically listed (scheduled) in the policy. If the auto is not scheduled, there is no coverage. Newly acquired autos are subject to specific restrictions and only a short period of "automatic coverage." However, to gain the 30 days of "automatic" protection granted, the insurance carrier must already insure all the insured's vehicles or the new vehicle must be a replacement for an existing auto. If the insurance carrier does not insure all the vehicles and the new vehicle is in addition to the current schedule, there is no automatic coverage on the vehicle and it is not covered until the insurer is notified of its existence. Symbol "7" is usually limited to physical damage protection, but it can be used to signify liability, uninsured/underinsured or physical damage.

Automobile Liability Laws and Limits

When reviewing the following information, remember the information was effective as of January 2010 and is subject to change.

Forty-nine states and the District of Columbia maintain compulsory liability insurance requirements. New Hampshire became the sole remaining voluntary financial responsibility state when Wisconsin's compulsory liability law took effect on June 2, 2010. However, uninsured motorist coverage is compulsory in New Hampshire.

In addition to compulsory auto liability coverage, some states require drivers to carry uninsured motorist coverage and others require drivers carry both uninsured (UM) and underinsured (UIM) motorist protection. Fifteen states plus the District of Columbia mandate uninsured motorist coverage for its drivers: Illinois, Kansas, Maryland, Massachusetts, New Hampshire, New Jersey, New York, North Dakota, Oregon, Rhode Island, South Carolina, South Dakota, Virginia and West Virginia. Only six states enforce compulsory uninsured AND underinsured motorist coverage protection; they are: Connecticut, Maine, Minnesota, North Carolina, Vermont and Wisconsin.

Personal Injury Protection (PIP), also known as "No Fault" protection, is the last major compulsory auto coverage law to which drivers may be subject. Sixteen states have compulsory PIP laws in place: Arkansas, Delaware, Florida, Hawaii, Kansas, Kentucky, Maryland, Massachusetts, Michigan, Minnesota, New Jersey, New York, North Dakota, Oregon, Pennsylvania and Utah. As is evidenced, PIP is very prevalent in the Northeast US. Drivers in 6 of the 11 states from Maryland through Maine operate subject to "no fault" statutes.

Chapter 18

Understanding the MCS-90

Although nearly 30 years has passed since its June 1981 introduction, the MCS-90 endorsement remains a highly misunderstood form. Apparent judicial misapplications of the intended meaning and purpose of the form have added to the confusion.

The MCS-90 was designed to assure that an at-fault "for-hire" (or public) motor carrier could fulfill its financial responsibility to the public, regardless of the insured's failure to comply with the underlying insurance policy's term and/or conditions. But it was not designed or intended to extend coverage to non-insureds or create coverage where none exists. Above all, the MCS-90 was not created to (and does not currently) provide any insurance coverage within the wording of the form. Insurance protection is extended only from the policy to which the endorsement is attached. The most current edition of the MCS-90 can easily be obtained on-line. You can go to the Federal Motor Carrier Safety Administration's website (www.fmcsa.dot.gov). Search "MCS-90" and this will give you a link to the downloadable form.

Attachment of the MCS-90 does nothing more than guarantee that there will be some source of funds available to pay for bodily injury, property damage or environmental restoration (collectively referred to as "public liability" in the MCS-90) made necessary by the negligence of the insured and its employees. However, this guarantee does not constitute insurance for one crucial reason: the insurance carrier issuing the MCS-90 has the right to recover from the entity named in the endorsement any payment made as a direct consequence of the provisions of the form.

In essence, the MCS-90 is more closely related to a surety bond guaranteeing that the insured has (and will continuously **maintain)** the coverage types and amounts mandated by law. And if the insured fails to **maintain** the required insurance coverage, the issuer of the MCS-90 will stand in the insured's place for the public good. But the issuer of the MCS-90 can and will likely seek full reimbursement from the insured named in the endorsement.

The Motor Carrier Regulatory Reform and Modernization Act, signed into law by President Jimmy Carter on July 1, 1980, was the impetus for the MCS-90 and requires motor carriers that transport hazardous materials to maintain "public liability" coverage of either $1 million or $5 million (depending on the material). As evidenced by the MCS-90's inclusion of "environmental restoration" within the definition of "public liability," the endorsement essentially guarantees that the motor carrier has pollution liability protection or a source of funds to cover a pollution loss as required by the law.

If, however, the motor carrier fails to maintain the required pollution coverage and there is a pollution loss, the MCS-90 issuing insurer will stand in place of the insured and pay the loss up to the legally required amount. But since the motor carrier failed to comply with the law, the insurer can then recover payment from the motor carrier.

To reiterate, the MCS-90 is not insurance. It is a financial guarantee protecting the public from the financial consequences of a motor carrier's failure to carry the statutorily required insurance protection. Any payment made solely under the provisions of the MCS-90 is recoverable from the defaulting motor carrier.

Remember, the burden to meet the statutory financial requirements placed on motor carriers engaged in interstate commerce is on the motor carrier, not the insurance carrier. When the MCS-90 is endorsed to a business auto policy, the insurance takes on two roles, the first as **insurer** and the second as **surety**. These competing requirements and roles coupled with the fact that a few of the "guarantees" provided by the MCS-90 are broader than the coverage provided by the underlying business auto policy (BAP) necessitates that the insurer carefully underwrite and confirm the underlying coverages that are to be maintained by the motor carrier.

Where the MCS-90 is Potentially Broader

- **Pollution:** Pollution losses are essentially excluded in the BAP. There are a few exceptions to the exclusions that do not extend to cover damage caused by materials being hauled. As stated in the above example, the MCS-90's definition of "public liability" includes environmental restoration – a pollution coverage. Since the insurance carrier issuing the MCS-90 has "guaranteed" that the motor carrier can pay for a pollution loss, it is incumbent upon the underwriter (and agent) to verify the necessary coverage.

- **Scheduled/Unscheduled Autos:** Business auto policies written on a "scheduled vehicle" basis can also be expanded by the attached MCS-90. The endorsement states that it covers all vehicles owned, operated or maintained by the insured "regardless of whether or not each motor vehicle is specifically described in the policy..." If the insured with a symbol "7" or "46" forgets to list or add a vehicle to the BAP, the insurer is normally not required to provide coverage for a loss. However, the MCS-90 negates this policy provision and requires the insurer to pay the loss. Since the insurer is acting as a surety in such a case, they may be able to recover from the insured.

- **Drivers:** The MCS-90 does not stipulate that individuals driving any vehicle or towing any trailer subject to the Motor Carrier Act be scheduled on the policy, qualify as an "insured" or even be considered "permitted users." In fact, the MCS-90 doesn't even address drivers, which has led to unique court rulings.

- **Cancellation:** Thirty-five day notice of cancellation is required by the endorsement, even for non-payment of premium. If the insured motor carrier is subject to Federal Motor Carrier Safety Administration registration, the FMCSA must get 30 day notice before the cancellation is effective. Here's the catch, the 30 days does not begin to toll until the FMCSA receives the cancellation notice in its Washington DC office. This is much longer than the standard notice of cancellation for non-payment of premium (between 10-15 days, based on state law), so the insurance carrier may be "on the hook" longer than required by the underlying BAP.

Court Decisions Can Alter the MCS-90's Intent and Purpose

John Deere Insurance Company v. Nueva (found on OpenJurist.org) expanded the MCS-90 definition of "insured" to include an entity that was not even a party (a "stranger") to the underlying BAP. The Ninth Circuit Court ruled that "insured" status under the MCS-90 extended to include an entity that had use of the named insured's trailer **after** it had been sold.

John Deere's insured (Baljit Singh Sahota DBA Sahota Trucking) sold a trailer to Gurmukh Garcha DBA Blue Star Transportation. Before the title of the trailer was transferred, it was involved in an at-fault accident cause by Blue Star. Even though Sahota no longer had possession of the trailer and was not a party to its use (contractual or otherwise), the court ruled that the provisions of the MCS-90 extended coverage to the trailer since the title had not passed. The purchaser became and "insured" on the policy per the court. In 2002, the Supreme Court issued an opinion that the Ninth Circuit's findings were incorrect, but at this point, the ruling stands as issued in 2000.

Deere v. Nueva is only one example of how courts can substantially alter the purpose and intent of the MCS-90. Some court rulings serve to cement the intended use of the endorsement. A recent Tenth District Court of Appeals case reversed and vacated 20 years of bad precedent in that district created by its 1989 finding in Empire Fire & Marine Ins. Co. v. Guaranty National Ins. Co.

Carolina Casualty Insurance Company v. Yeates saw the Tenth District court in California join the majority opinion in stating that the MCS-90 does not create coverage in an underlying BAP where no coverage existed. In fact, the court laid out two tests that must be satisfied before the MCS-90 can be called upon to respond to a loss.

- The underlying [auto] insurance policy to which the endorsement is attached does not provide coverage for the motor carrier's accident.
- The motor carrier's insurance coverage is either not sufficient to satisfy the federally prescribed minimum levels of financial responsibility or is non-existent.

Conclusion

The intent of the MCS-90 appears rather self-evident on its surface; it is not insurance, simply a safety net for innocent parties injured by the negligence of the named insured. However, sympathetic juries and judges have expanded the protection turning this safety net into a pseudo insurance policy.

Knowing how the form is designed to work should allow agents to effectively explain the need for the endorsement to the insured, beyond just, "because the government requires it." Also, being able to provide the necessary underlying protection will serve your client and make the underwriter more comfortable with the risk.

Chapter 19

Understanding Reinsurance

Reinsurance in the simplest terms is insurance for insurance companies. Primary insurance carriers "cede" (place with) some portion of the risks they agree to underwrite (based on the design of the reinsurance contract) to a reinsurance carrier which is known as the "cedant." Primary insurers and reinsurers negotiate and re-negotiate these contracts based on market conditions, trends and loss history.

Negotiated reinsurance contracts influence the breadth of (or even the limit on) risks primary insurance carriers can (and are willing to) underwrite. The primary insurer's capacity and "appetite" is proportional to the availability and use of reinsurance: the lower the reinsurer's capacity, the lower the primary insurer's capacity; and the narrower the reinsurer's appetite, the narrower the appetite of the primary insurer.

Retrocession is reinsurance for the reinsurer. The reinsurer has agreed to take on risks from several primary insurers and they, in turn, place some of their financial risks with other reinsurance carriers. The number of insurance carriers, primary, reinsurers and retrocessionaires (the reinsurer of the reinsurer) on a block of risks may be surprising.

Reinsurance is vital to the entire insurance mechanism, especially in light of the global insurance economy. Reinsurance accomplishes five functions/goals.

1. Stabilizes the earnings of the primary insurer in the event of catastrophic losses
2. Increases the primary insurer's capacity by limiting its liability on individual risks
3. Provides liquidity and protects against swings in business cycles
4. Provides underwriting expertise to the primary insurer
5. Can partially protect the insured in the event of a primary insurer's insolvency

What follows is a quick synopsis of some parts of the reinsurance mechanism. This is a high-level overview of reinsurance relationships and contracts. Contracts can be individually negotiated based on these rules of construction.

Facultative vs. Treaty Reinsurance

Primary insurers and reinsurers negotiate reinsurance contracts utilizing facultative agreements, treaty agreementsor often a combination of the two. Each agreement serves a particular purpose.

Facultative Reinsurance: Can be defined and easily recalled remembering the term *"facilitative."* Facultative reinsurance is reinsurance for a single risk or a defined package of risks. The ceding company (the primary insurer) is not compelled to submit these risks to the reinsurer, but neither is the reinsurer compelled to provide reinsurance protection. Each risk under a facultative contract is individually underwritten by the reinsurer. The agreement to provide reinsurance "facilitates" the primary insurer's desire to write the business. Without the reinsurance, the primary insurer may be unable to provide coverage for the agent.

A good example of the use of facultative reinsurance is a property risk with a very high total insurable value (TIV, or Maximum Possible Loss). The primary insurer does not, of its own resources and appetite, have the capacity to provide the requested limits. To provide the coverage, the primary insurer submits the risk to the reinsurer to facilitate (allow) the coverage. If the reinsurer agrees, coverage is written and a facultative reinsurance contract is created.

Treaty Reinsurance: A pre-negotiated agreement between the primary insurer and the reinsurer. The primary insurer agrees to cede all risks within a defined class or classes to the reinsurer. In return, the reinsurer agrees to provide reinsurance on all risks ceded without individual underwriting. "Underwriting" is done during negotiation of the treaty contract, thus none is done at the time of the cession.

Pro-Rata vs. Excess of Loss Reinsurance

Facultative and Treaty Reinsurance contracts can be designed utilizing pro-rata or excess of loss provisions. Both pro-rata and excess of loss reinsurance contracts can be further broken down into sub-categories.

Pro-Rata Reinsurance: The primary insurer cedes a predetermined percentage of the risk to the reinsurer. The reinsurer shares in the losses proportional to the premiums and limits reinsured. Two major types of pro-rata reinsurance are "quota share" and "surplus share."

- *Quota share agreements* require the primary insurer to cede a certain percentage of every risk within the agreement to the reinsurer paying a proportional premium for the transfer of risk. In return, the reinsurer agrees to indemnify losses suffered by the ceding company in the same proportion. If, for example, the reinsurer agrees to reinsure 35% of the risk (accepting a proportional premium for that agreement), they pay 35% of any losses.

- *Surplus share agreements* allow the primary insurer to cede a negotiated percentage of liabilities over a pre-determined retention. The ceded amount is usually greater than the amount retained by the primary insurer. Premiums and losses above the retention are received and paid by the reinsurer in the same proportion. For example, the primary insurer agrees to pay the first $100 million dollars on a certain block of business, but negotiates to cede 70% of all losses above $100 million to the reinsurer. If the block experiences $500 million in losses during the contract period, the primary insurer pays the first $100 million plus 30% of the remaining $400 million for a total of

$220 million. The reinsurer is on the hook for 70% of the $400 million or $280 million.

Excess of Loss Reinsurance: The reinsurer agrees to indemnify the primary insurer for all (not a percentage of) losses exceeding a specified retention either on a per loss basis or an aggregate loss basis. Catastrophe reinsurance, per risk reinsurance, per occurrence reinsurance and aggregate excess of loss reinsurance are all categories of excess of loss reinsurance.

- **Catastrophic reinsurance contracts** indemnify the ceding company for all losses in excess of a specified amount resulting from a single catastrophic event.

- **Per risk reinsurance contracts** apply to individual risks (most likely part of a facultative agreement) whereby the reinsurer agrees to assume losses over a pre-determined amount. The primary insurer pays all losses up to that point.

- **Per occurrence reinsurance contracts** are similar to catastrophe reinsurance.

- **Aggregate excess of loss reinsurance contracts** stipulate that the reinsurer will pay ALL primary insurer losses that exceed a specified retention during the contract period. For example, the primary insurer contracts with the reinsurer to insure aggregate losses exceeding $500 million in the period. This primary insurer is indemnified for all loss payments above that amount (subject to the policy limit).

Pro-rata and excess of loss contracts are often used in tandem by the primary insurance carrier utilizing several reinsurers to secure long-term financial viability.

Solvency and Reinsurance Contracts

There are provisions within (and endorsements to) reinsurance contracts that revolve around the potential for financial problems, either the primary insurer's financial downfall or the slippage of the reinsurer. Two of these contractual provisions are the Cut-Through Endorsement and the Downgrade Clause.

Cut-Through Endorsement: An endorsement regarding payment of reinsurance attached to either the reinsurance contract or underlying contract activated by the insolvency of the primary insurer. The endorsement stipulates that any payment the reinsurer would have made to the primary insurer goes directly to the insured or third-party beneficiary (in a liability situation). Note that this does not guarantee the payment of the entire loss, just the amount that the reinsurer would have paid to indemnify the primary insurer. A pro rata agreement in which the reinsurer agrees to indemnify the primary insurer 40% of any loss, for example, would only pay 40% of the loss to the insured. In essence, the insured or third-party beneficiary steps into the shoes of the insolvent primary insurer and is entitled to the amount that would have been paid to the insurance company. Very few insureds possess the underwriting "clout" to demand or qualify for a cut-through endorsement. However, a "cut-through **clause**" in the policy, not added by endorsement and not specific to a particular insured, would apply to all insureds. Some reinsurance experts advise against the use of cut-through endorsement clauses for various legal, contractual and financial reasons.

Downgrade Clause: Primary insurers (cedants) may desire to protect themselves against any financial downturn of the reinsurance carrier with whom they have contracted. The provisions of the downgrade clause allow the primary insurer to require the reinsure to bolster their financial condition in the event of a downturn. If that is not done, or it is not sufficient, and the reinsurer's financial rating falls below a certain point, the cedant can withdraw from the reinsurance contract (expecting the return of all unused premium). Reinsurance experts state that such clauses are detrimental to reinsurers.

Reportedly, many reinsurers (especially those awash in cash and financially very strong) are resisting providing such provisions in their contracts.

Conclusion

Reinsurance is vital to the insurance mechanism as it exists today. Capacity and risk appetite are based on the capital provided by reinsurers and the contractual agreements between primary insurers and reinsurers.

Chapter 20

How to Insure Joint Ventures

A joint venture (JV) is a separate entity formed by the teaming of two or more persons or entities for the purpose of engaging in an activity or operation with the intention of earning a profit (or accomplishing some other goal). Each member of the joint venture has an equity stake in that each shares in the venture's income and expenses at some pre-negotiated level. Generally one member of the JV is the managing member responsible for making final business decisions regarding the operation of the joint venture (for this additional duty, they are often paid a fee or some additional remuneration). More in-depth information on legal particulars of joint ventures is outside the scope of this chapter and expertise of its author.

Design and implementation of a joint venture's insurance program is based on the JV's legal structure, the agreement between or among the JV members and, in part, on the purpose for which the joint venture is created. Three keys to planning a joint venture insurance program are: 1) choosing which of the three available insurance options to apply, 2) assuring that the chosen insurance program accomplishes two main goals, and 3) considering the JV's eventual demise in the planning of the insurance program.

Legal Structure

Joint ventures can be set up as a partnership, limited partnership or corporation. Regardless of the chosen legal structure, the result is a separate legal entity. The power or ability of any one member of the joint venture to legally bind other members to specific commitments rests in the legal structure.

Just as in any other insured entity, the legal status of a joint venture affects certain coverages, most notably, the workers' compensation policy.

A Joint Venture's Purpose

Why was the joint venture created? Was it created to "conduct an activity" such as developing property for a residential area, commercial office park, industrial complex or some other like project? Or was the JV created to combine the resources and talents of compatible industries to run an operation? An example of "running an operation" may include a supplier and manufacturer forming a joint venture and opening a plant to produce a product more efficiently than the market as a whole.

Whether the JV is created to conduct an activity or run an operation will likely dictate the resources contributed by each member of the venture. "Man power" and time may be all that is required to conduct an activity, where running an operation likely requires the addition of a plant and equipment to the venture. The breadth of resources contributed to the venture directly relates to which of the three insurance options (listed below) is the best choice.

Two Goals of a JV Insurance Program

Although a bit out of order, understanding the two goals of a joint venture insurance program is necessary to adequately analyze the three common options for insuring a joint venture.

Since a properly formed joint venture is a distinct legal entity separate from its founding members, it has the rights of any other person or entity. Among these is the right to sue, be sued and recover from any entity that causes it harm, including the founding members.

Because of the "rights" afforded to the joint venture, **severability and removing the ability of one carrier to subrogate against any member of the joint venture** are the two insurance program goals that must be accomplished. Regardless of which of the three insurance options is chosen the ultimate program requires the use of proper forms and endorsements necessary to assure severability and non-subrogation among the various entities.

Accomplishing these goals is a balancing act. Each entity must be held responsible for its own actions without limiting or negating the availability of coverage for any other entity (severability). At the same time, because the joint venture and its members are contractually conjoined, the ability of one member to recover from another member tends to violate the spirit of a joint venture – the sharing of revenues and liabilities as established in the founding agreement, thus the need to remove subrogation rights.

Joint Venture Insurance Options

Joint ventures, as separate and individual legal entities, require insurance protection just like any other entity. However, the options for securing the necessary protection are broader than those available to most other insured operations. Three main options exist for managing the insurance exposures created by a joint venture.

1. Each member insures its own exposure created by the joint venture under existing coverage (via alteration of their own policies).
2. One member insures the joint venture in totality.
3. The joint venture procures its own insurance.

Each Member Insures its Own Risk

This may be the least beneficial option for every member involved. First, use of this option is viable only when there is limited investment by the member parties; essentially limited to "man power" and time. Basically this is a viable option when the JV is created with the sole purpose of conducting an activity on a short-term basis. This option would not work well if there is shared use of property or equipment.

Use of this option requires several specific endorsements to both the commercial general liability (CGL) and workers' compensation (WC) policies.

Commercial General Liability: CGL policies specifically exclude joint ventures, even if newly formed, which are not specifically listed as a named insured. Each member forming the JV must first specifically endorse the CGL naming the joint venture as an insured. And, to accomplish the second JV coverage goal (waiving subrogation), each member should attach the Additional Insured – Designated Person or Organization (CG 20 26) to the CGL naming the other members of the JV as additional insureds.

Workers Compensation: Because a properly created joint venture is essentially a separate legal entity, employees of any members working for (or on behalf of) the JV may be considered "borrowed servants" of the venture even though they are not its direct employees. If the joint venture has none of its own employee and is not required by the subject jurisdiction to provide WC, each member would protect the joint venture by attaching the Alternate Employer Endorsement (WC 00 03 01 A) to its policy, naming the joint venture as the alternate employer. This option would not be available if the joint venture is required by the jurisdiction in question to provide its own coverage as a direct "employer" rather than a "special" employer.

Secondly, each member would attach a Waiver of our Right to Recover from Other Endorsements (WC 00 03 13) in favor of the other members. Combining these endorsements ensures that the employee is compensated and none of the members are held liable for any injury they may have caused to another member's employee.

One Member Insures the Joint Venture in Totality

The specifics of this option are varied based on the agreement between or among the members. If the member responsible for providing coverage chooses to add the joint venture to its own policy, essentially the same steps detailed above should be followed. However, if the member chooses to place separate coverage, the steps delineated below will apply. Any combination of these may be used if this option is chosen.

The Joint Venture Procures its Own Insurance

As a separate legal entity, this may be the most appropriate option of the three. Beyond being the cleanest choice for protecting the joint venture, there are other advantages for each of the members.

- Loss experience is assigned to the joint venture rather than the members.
- Losses caused by the JV do not affect the limits of coverage available to the members.
- Claims are handled by one carrier rather than potentially several.
- The members of the JV can be named as additional insureds on the joint venture's policy rather than the reverse (as in option 1 above).
- Only one call is necessary to request a certificate of insurance or report a claim.

Another advantage of separate coverage is the breadth of protection that can be procured. This is the best method when the joint venture is formed to "run an operation." The "operation" exposure may include plant, property or equipment. Trying to insure these on individual member policies can be cumbersome.

Commercial General Liability. As stated above, the joint venture should name each member as an additional insured to protect them from vicarious liability for the actions of the JV. The same CG 20 26 discussed in option 1 should be used. Reciprocally, each member should name the other members as additional insureds to protect each from the actions of the other (accomplishing the second goal of JV insurance). The same CG 20 26 can be used, being careful to specifically limit the additional insured status to apply only to liability arising out of the activities of the joint venture. The JV should probably not be added as an additional insured to the individual member's policies as this has the potential to severely hamper the application of the "Other Insurance" condition in the CGL. Each member may want to name the JV on their own CGL to provide an excess layer of protection should the JV's limits not be sufficient.

Workers Compensation. Direct employees of the joint venture can be insured on a separate workers' compensation policy in the name of the joint venture. The only required modification is attachment of the Joint Venture as Insured Endorsement (WC 00 03 05). This endorsement limits coverage to the employees of the joint venture and specifically excludes coverage for employees of the member companies. Joint ventures are eligible for experience rating based on the mathematical averages of the experience modification factors of the member companies in the beginning. Once the joint venture has existed long enough on its own, a mod for the JV is calculated.

Dissolution of the Joint Venture

Rarely do joint ventures run into perpetuity, thus planning the insurance protection necessary to protect the members following the JV's eventual demise must be planned. The options for insuring a prior joint venture are essentially the same as those available for providing coverage during the JV's existence.

Liability Coverages: If the members choose to individually insure the post-closure products or completed operations exposures of the joint venture, they must remember to specifically name the JV as an insured on the CGL. However, the members do have the option to continue insuring the defunct JV separately by attaching a proprietary or manuscripted discontinued operations endorsement to the JV's policy. Also, if any coverage was provided to the joint venture on a "claims made" basis, a decision regarding the purchase of a supplemental extended reporting period must be made.

Workers' Compensation and Other Coverages: Because the entity to which these coverages were assigned no longer exists, neither does the need for coverage. The workers' compensation policy can be cancelled and any property or other such policies can likewise be cancelled. Loss experience attributable to the joint venture stays with the joint venture and does not transfer to the members once the JV shutters.

Finishing Up

Joint ventures are unique entities requiring study and understanding. Entity type, member agreement and purpose make each JV different from every other one. This chapter is not intended to discuss every possible coverage needed by any particular joint venture, rather it provides a basic overview of the insurance process used to evaluate coverage for a joint venture.

Chapter 21

Understanding the Dos and Don'ts of E&O Threats

Ask any agent who has suffered through an errors and omissions (E&O) suit and they will provide sage-like insight into the professional and even personal trials created by such an ordeal. I recently met an agent whose agency closed the last of 16 E&O suits related to Hurricane Katrina four years after the storm. His newfound experience is priceless (although he hopes to never have to call on that experience).

Proper actions and reactions once threatened or served with an E&O suit are of utmost importance. Once a threat is made, or a suit filed, the allegedly improper act or omission has already occurred – don't make the situation worse by making bad decisions.

The dos and don'ts of an E&O claim are often discussed in errors and omissions courses sponsored by the agency's professional liability insurance carriers, state associations or agency consultants. Many agency consultants can perform agency audits to help prevent, as much as possible, E&O situations and prepare an agency for responding when one comes. Following are just some general "do" and "don't" tips that may need to be customized to fit a particular agency.

First – You DON'T

The first big "don't" is, **do not overreact to the claim.** Understand that there is NO shame in being pulled into an E&O situation. Even the best agents and agencies are open to an E&O claim, regardless of the procedures and protections in place to avoid them. Take the experience, learn from it and make the necessary changes to assure that no such situation arises again. Anger at yourself or others is counterproductive and can increase the weight of the situation. Once you have the proper perspective, focus on these other "don'ts".

- ***Do not, under any circumstances, alter the client's file as it relates to the charges.*** Do not add details, delete details, or change details. Such changes are easily found in electronic files, and even if paper files are used, any changes can be evident. Making any changes creates the appearance that there is something to hide.

- ***Do not discuss the claim with anyone other than the claims representative, defense attorney or any other member of the office DIRECTLY involved in the claim.*** Comments made under duress or when angry can be misconstrued and be potentially damaging in court if such comments are recounted on the stand. The only individuals that need to be involved in any discussion of the case are those in the office directly related to the care of the plaintiff's account and those defending the agency.

- ***Do not make any admission of liability or wrongdoing and do not offer or make payment***. This is the same advice agents give their clients when involved in an auto accident. Allow the legal process, and those hired to debate and decide questions of law, make the determination of legal liability and amount of damages.

- ***Do not provide any written or recorded statement to the plaintiff without your carrier's claims representative present.*** Since this will be admissible, the agent will want guidance on how to truthfully give an account of the story using facts without unnecessary opinion or emotion.

- ***Do not allow inspection, copying or removal of client files and records without consulting with the claims representative managing the claim.*** This is the agency's information about the client, not necessarily the client's information. The claims representative needs to know what information is being requested and what is not.

- ***Do not try to manage the claim on your own.*** The E&O carrier has more experience and is better able to manage the process. Remember, other clients must be cared for, new business must be written and the agency must be managed. Allow those with more experience, time and resources to take care of the agency.

What to DO

The list of "dos" seem almost like common sense, but they still require mention. Following are a few of the immediate and ongoing "dos" of E&O.

- ***Notify the E&O carrier of a "claim" at once.***
  Provisions in the errors and omissions policy require the insured to notify the insurance carrier as soon as practicable upon the receipt of a "claim." A "claim" is a defined term that can mean something as innocent as a threat, or a letter from the insured or the actual suit papers. It's incumbent upon the agent to know the definition of a "claim" in its policy and notify the carrier in compliance with that definition.

- ***Gather and organize all pertinent records related to the insured and the situation.*** But in doing so, remember the "don't" number "2;" don't alter them. The claims representative will need all the information to conduct an investigation and prepare and provide a proper defense.

- ***Write down all the information known about the incident surrounding the claim.*** Each member of the team directly related to the client and the incident giving rise to the E&O claim should record all they can remember about the incident or incidents on which the claim is based. This should be a factual narrative statement in chronological order.

- ***Cooperate with the E&O carrier.*** This includes providing information and facts that look bad for the agency. Hiding or hedging certain aspects of the facts surrounding the situation on which the claim is based creates distrust between you and your insurer. It also makes you look guilty. The insurer is on your side.

- ***Make sure you comply with all policy conditions and requirements.*** If the agency fails to comply with all E&O policy conditions, coverage may be jeopardized.

Hopefully It Will Never Happen to You

This is a quick recap of some of the more common "dos" and "don'ts" and is not a complete list of all that will be required at the time of a claim. Your insurance carrier will ask for information and may require some actions not contained in this list.

As stated, hopefully this information will be superfluous for your agency. However, this is still good information for you in advising your professional liability clients in the event they suffer an E&O or professional liability claim.

Appendix A

Glossary of Terms

"A Priori" Data

Prediction about the probability of a future event based on deductive reasoning rather than trials, tests or even history. This is essentially an exercise in mathematical calculation based on known data (and all the factors must be known). A priori calculations cannot guarantee the outcome, only that the outcome can be predicted with a reasonable amount of certainty.

Abandonment of Employment

Engaging in an activity clearly not intended for the advancement of the employer nor directed by or anticipated by the employer. Includes any activity in direct contradiction to the rules, requests or expectations of the employer.

Accident

Accident carries with it the implied application of being definite in time and place and being unintended.

Accrual Basis of Accounting

Per the IRS: Under an accrual method of accounting, income is reported in the year it is earned and expenses are deducted or capitalized in the year incurred.

Actual Cash Value (ACV)

ACV is the cost new (replacement cost) on the date of the loss minus physical depreciation.

Adverse Selection

Originally coined by the insurance industry to explain the cause of upwardly spiraling pricing resulting from worsening loss histories directly proportional to the deteriorating risk characteristics of those insured. Academically, this is referred to as the "adverse selection death spiral." The most basic definition of adverse selection is that the insurance company is chosen against by those most likely to suffer loss.

Agent

An agent contractually and statutorily represents the insurance carrier as its principal. The law of contract gives the agent the right to represent the insurance company and act on its behalf to solicit and bind coverage. Insurance carriers are usually bound by the actions of their agent provided the agent acts within the bounds of the agency contract. Regardless of how an agent tries to position himself/herself, they most act in the best interest of the insurance carrier (act as a fiduciary) in the placement of coverage, the solicitation of business, and in the settlement of claims.

Alien Carrier

An insurance carrier incorporated and domiciled in another country but operating in the US.

Allocated Loss Adjustment Expense (ALAE)

Loss adjustment costs assignable to a particular loss and not attributable to the overall cost of providing loss adjusting services. The cost of outside investigation, appraisal and defense counsel are examples of ALAE.

All In

Used in reference to condominiums, sometimes referred to as "all-inclusive." The association is responsible for insuring common elements, limited common elements and unit-only real property. Unit improvements and betterments are also insured by the association.

All Normal Operating Expenses (ANOE)

Operating expenses that would have been incurred had no business-closing loss occurred.

Altruism

Altruism is putting others above yourself; letting their interest take precedent over your self-interest. Altruism does not expect any rewards or recognition for the good that is done. It is motivated purely by the good of the other person. Altruism is the first of the nine Canons of a CPCU (which at one point had to be memorized).

Amount Subject to Loss

Maximum Coinsurance Percentage x 12 months business income calculation.

Arising out of...

A casual connection between the furtherance of the employer's business and the injury. If the employer benefits in some way from the activity, then the injury or illness suffered in the pursuit of that activity is considered to arise out of the employment.

Assault

No actual bodily contract, only the threat of bodily injury by force. Such threat is intentional and unlawfully directed towards another person such that the other party has a reasonable fear that injury is likely to occur. The apparent ability to carry out such a threat must also exist. (See Battery)

Assumption of Risk

A defense against charges of negligence barring or severely limiting an individual's recovery under the tort of negligence. The defendant must prove that 1) the plaintiff was reasonably aware of and appreciated the danger involved, 2) the plaintiff voluntarily exposed himself to the danger, and 3) the assumed danger was the proximate cause of the injury or damage.

Bare Walls

Used in relation to condominiums. Associational insurance requirements are limited to common elements and limited common elements.

Basement (NFIP)

Any area of the building, including any sunken room or sunken portion of a room, having its floor below ground level (sub-grade) on all sides.

Batch Clause

A batch clause limits the amount of coverage to the per occurrence limits for all defective products that come from a single run or batch. These batch clauses are generally found only in proprietary or manuscript forms.

Professional liability policies often are subject to a batch-type clause, however these clauses generally relate to the deductible or retention. Multiple suits arising out of the same "wrongful act" do not subject the insured to separate deductibles (or retention). Only one deductible is applied to all suits that result from the same wrongful act.

Battery

Actual physical contact with another individual resulting in physical injury. Such contact is not limited to physical beating but can also refer to physical restraint of a person. Battery can exist without assault.

Bodily Injury

Bodily Injury from an insurance standpoint means bodily harm, sickness or disease sustained by a person, including death resulting from any of these at any time. Mental anguish and loss of service is, at times, included as part of this definition depending on the jurisdiction.

Breakaway Walls

Non-structural walls perpendicular to the flow of water (takes the direct hit) designed to fail under certain wave force conditions. The failure of these walls should cause NO damage to the structural supports, the foundation or any part of the building above the walls.

Broad Transfer

Provides the greatest scope of contractual risk transfer and requires the transferee to indemnify and hold harmless the transferor from all liability arising out of an incident, even if the act is committed solely by the transferor. This may qualify as an exculpatory contract and is illegal in some jurisdictions because the wording is considered "unconscionable."

Broker

A broker represents the insurance buyer as its principle in the negotiation of coverage. A broker cannot bind the insurance carrier to anything, nor do they speak on behalf of the insurance carrier. Brokers can only negotiate and speak on behalf of the insured in the placement of coverage. Brokers are to act in the best interest of the client (the insured) in the placement of coverage and claims settlement.

Business Income

Net profit or loss that would have been earned plus continuing normal operating expenses.

Casual Labor

Work that is not in the usual course of trade, business, occupation or profession of the employer (contracting party). Essentially, a casual laborer is one that does not directly promote or advance the employers business or operation.

Causal Nexus

A legal term that in Latin means "to bind." Legally it means to link a cause and effect. A causal nexus exists if the result is a natural and reasonable outcome or consequence of the activity. This does not equate to or require the same level of connection as does "proximate cause" (the idea that a result would not have occurred "but for" the actions of the person).

Chattel

Movable or immovable, tangible or intangible personal property. Chattel does not include real estate or structures attached to the real estate.

Clawback Provisions

Legalized by the Sarbanes-Oxley Act of 2002 (Section 304), this provision is included in a growing number of executive employment contracts. These provisions allow boards of directors to demand repayment of performance-based bonuses made to CEO's and CFO's if such bonuses were paid based on fraud or misstatements in financial information.

Collateral Estoppel

A judgment of fact found in one case prevents a party from trying to deny that fact in another case. The parties are permanently bound by the prior ruling. If Elliot Spitzer were tried and found guilty of malicious prosecution in his criminal trial (a question of "fact"), he would be estopped (collaterally) from denying guilt in any trial that follows. His guilt would be considered a foregone conclusion decided by a previous jury and undeniable in any succeeding case (example only, not intended to imply or suggest any actual suit).

Combustible Liquids

Liquids having a closed cup flash point equal to or greater than 100 degrees Fahrenheit. These liquids are divided into Class II and Class III.

- *Class II liquids* – flash points at or above 100 degrees Fahrenheit and below 140 degrees Fahrenheit
- *Class IIIA liquids* – flash points at or above 140 degrees Fahrenheit and below 200 degrees Fahrenheit
- *Class IIIB liquids* – flash points at or above 200 degrees Fahrenheit

Coming and Going Rule

Injury suffered traveling to or home from work or even while going to and returning from lunch is generally not compensable. The logic behind the rule is that the employee is not furthering the employer's interest or serving the business' needs.

Common Elements (Condominiums)

Common elements are owned by and benefit all members of the association. Land, parking lots, each building's structural foundations and load-bearing walls are examples of common elements. Also included in this definition are club houses, pool houses, pools, fences, gates, playground equipment, tennis courts and other property owned and allocated to all unit owners. Not all property categorized as a common element is insurable in standard property policies, but most can be scheduled.

Comparative Negligence

Each party's relative "fault" for the subject accident is compared. The insured party's (plaintiff's) ultimate damage award is reduced by his percentage of culpability. Three variations of the comparative fault rule are utilized across the US. In each variation, the damaged party's award is reduced by the percentage of their own contribution to the incident:

- *Pure Comparative Fault*: Allows the damaged party to recover even if they are 99% at fault. Thirteen states apply this rule of comparative negligence: AK, AZ, CA, FL, KY, LA, MS, MO, NM, NY, RI, SD, WA
- *Modified Comparative – 50% Bar:* A damaged party cannot recover if they are 50% or more at fault. They are able to recover from 0% to 49% at fault. Twelve states apply this rule of comparative negligence: AR, CO, GA, ID, KS, ME, NE, OK, TN, UT, WV
- *Modified Comparative – 51% Bar:* A damaged party can recover from another party provided they are no more than 50% at fault. Twenty-one states apply this version of comparative negligence: CT, DE, HI, IL, IN, IA, MA, MI, MN, MT, NV, NH, NJ, OH, OR, PA, SC, TX, VT, WI, WY

Compensable Business Income

The actual amount of business income paid during the period of restoration necessary to indemnify the insured. This may be less than the **insurable business income** because it is based on net profit or loss plus actual on-going (continuing) expenses incurred during the period of restoration.

Compensatory Damages

Payment for actual injury or economic loss. Divided into Special Damages and General Damages. Special Damages are specific and quantifiable (i.e. medical costs, lost wages, repair cost, etc.). General Damages "generally" have no basis for calculation and include pain and suffering, mental anguish or loss of reputation.

Concealment

A lie by omission; to prevent information from being known. Improving the perception of something by withholding truth that may change a decision. If the underwriter had wanted to know, he/she would have asked. Concealment may actually be an unintentional act. The concealment of a material fact results in a policy becoming void.

Constructive Total Loss

The property can be repaired, but the cost to repair the damaged property is greater than the value of the property once it is repaired (it would cost more to repair it than it would be worth when done).

Continuing (Normal) Operating Expenses

Normal operating expenditures that continue (in whole or in part) during the time the operations are discontinued due to a direct property loss (the "Period of Restoration").

Contract

A formal agreement between two or more parties' intent on accomplishing a specific task, purpose or goal. Agreements can encompass the performance of an act or acts, or an agreement to refrain from some particular deed. Specific duties are created by contract and contracts are subject to their own set of laws.

Contract of Hire

Contract of hire states approach the issue of extraterritorial jurisdiction and when to name a 3.A. state from the employment contract standpoint. The vast majority of states statutorily subscribe to this approach.

Contractual Risk Transfer

A formal agreement between two parties whereby one agrees to indemnify and hold another party harmless for specified acts. Such transfer encompasses both Risk Financing (planning for the cost of a loss) and Risk Control (developing means to avoid or lessen the cost of a loss). The intended goal of contractual risk transfer is to place the financial burden of a loss on the party best able to control and prevent the loss.

Contributing Location

A dependent property location that supplies the insured with the parts, materials or services necessary to manufacture its product or provide its service (suppliers).

Contributory Negligence

Doctrine of defense stating that if the injured person was even partially culpable in causing or aggravating his own injury he is barred from any recovery from the other party. This is an absolute defense.

COPE

Information used by property underwriters to analyze and price a particular risk.

- **Construction** – Construction can be broken down into three major sub-groups: 1) construction materials – wood, masonry, metal, etc., 2) square footage, and 3) age of the structure.

- **Occupancy** – Each operation within a building presents a unique hazard and distinct risk of loss. The relative risk of loss presented by a particular operation is a basis for the final property rate. Similar occupancy classes present individualized "hazards of occupancy" that are also analyzed.

- **Protection** – Protection includes the steps that are being taken and the services offered to protect the property from loss (i.e. sprinkler systems, fire extinguishers, alarm systems and public fire protection.

- **Exposures** – These are external factors beyond the insured's control. What is adjacent to the risk? Are there any unique operations within the same building that could increase the risk of loss? Is the building

located in a seismic zone, special flood hazard area
(SFHA) or high-wind area?

Crumbling Skull

A legal theory sometimes used as a defense to or argument
against application of the **Eggshell Skull** rule. The principle
behind this defense is that the result would have been the same
whether or not the accused wrongdoer was involved. The best
examples appear in medical practices. The patient was dying,
the doctor attempted some radical measures to save his life
and did not succeed and in fact the actions were the proximate
cause of death. Crumbling skull principles would not hold the
doctor responsible for causing a foregone conclusion. To
protect the doctor, the death would have to have been certain
within approximately the same time frame.

Cut-Through Endorsement

An endorsement relating to the payment of reinsurance
proceeds and attached to either the primary insurance contract
or the reinsurance contract activated by the insolvency of the
primary insurer. The endorsement stipulates that any payment
the reinsure would have made to the primary insurer goes
directly to the insured. Note, this does not guarantee the
payment of the entire loss, just the amount that the reinsurer
would have paid to indemnify the primary insurer.

Damages

Damages serve a dual purpose: 1) as a monetary remedy for a person, persons or entity against which a wrong has been committed and/or an injury suffered. The remedy may only be a part of 2) the total sum imposed on a tortfeasor for their violation of a duty owed.

Before damages are imposed there must be a duty owed or created (tort, contract or statute), a breach and a resulting injury. There are several types of damages: **Compensatory Damages, Punitive Damages and Liquidated Damages.**

Dangerous Instrumentality Doctrine

An absolute/strict liability ownership doctrine. This doctrine does not require any particular conduct, merely the presence of something that could cause harm. The basis of this doctrine is rooted in property rights. Owners and occupiers of land have the right to expect peaceful and safe enjoyment of the property they occupy. Adjacent property owners have the duty (responsibility) to use and maintain their land in such a way as to protect the surrounding owner's rights. Owners or occupier of land who store or maintain a dangerous instrumentality are held strictly liable for any injury that occurs because of the exposure to an unreasonable risk of harm.

De Facto Employee

De facto means "in fact" or "in reality." The degree of control often influences the workers' classification as a true independent contractor or a de facto employee.

De Jure Employee

De jure means "by right, according to the law." A de jure employee is an employee created by an act of law. In most states, injured employees of an uninsured subcontractor become the responsibility of the general contractor; they become the "de jure employees" of the general contractor by action of workers' compensation law.

Derivative Suit

Derivative suits are brought by one or several shareholders on behalf of a publically held corporation. It derives out of the shareholders perceived mismanagement of the corporation by an individual or several members of the directors or officers.

Diminution of Value

The difference in the fair market value of personal property (chattel) following damage and repair, and what the property would have been worth had no damage occurred.

Discretionary Payroll

Payroll expenses of specified individuals or classes of employees whose services are not necessary to resume operations.

Doctrinal Employer-Employee Relationship (Special Employer)

1) The direct employer volunteered or directed the employee to work for the special employer and has the employee agree to such assignment; 2) the work being done essentially that of the special employer; and 3) the special employer has the right to control the details of the work.

Domestic Carrier

A carrier operating in the state in which it is incorporated.

Dual Purpose Operation

Operations that receive income from both manufacturing and non-manufacturing operations which are not directly relatable to the manufacturing process.

Eggshell Skull

A legal term based in tort and criminal law that states that tortfeasors take the injured party as they find them. Also known as the "think skull rule", it states that if the injured party has a condition that predisposes them to greater injury than the normal human, the tortfeasor is not relieved of any of the costs resulting from the increased bodily injury just because of the condition. All injury and the costs associated with such injuries are assigned to the individual that committed the initial wrongful act, regardless of the ability to foresee the results or the fact that the injury is made worse by a pre-existing condition or predisposition to injury.

Elevated Building (NFIP)

A non-basement building with its lowest elevated floor raised above ground level by foundation walls, shear walls, posts, piers, pilings, or columns.

Empirical Data

Predictions about future events depend on data gathered from past events. It is trying to predict the future based on what has happened in the past. Also known as "a posteriori" data.

Employee

A person hired to perform certain services or tasks for particular wages or salary under the control of another (the employer), or a worker hired to perform a specific job usual and customary to the employer's business operation in exchange for money or other remuneration.

Equitable Estoppel

Prevents a person from adopting a new position that contradicts a previous position created by words, silence, or actions if allowing the adoption of the new position would unfairly harm the person who relied on the previous position to his or her detriment. Also known as "estoppel in pais."

Escheat

A common law doctrine to assure that unclaimed property of an individual that dies intestate is not left without an owner. In modern terms, escheat simply means that the property of an intestate without living heirs (see **Intestacy**) passes to the state. If an heir within the state's definition is later found, property can be reclaimed by that individual. Escheat statutes generally govern the procedure that must be undertaken to find a rightful heir. If the effort is unsuccessful, the property is to be used for the public good. The burden of proof that there is no rightful heir falls on the state, with all rules of evidence applicable. Property of veterans that die intestate reverts to the Federal government.

Estoppel

Simply means to stop, block or not allow a party to take a new position that contradicts previous actions or conditions upon which an expectation was created and ultimately to their detriment. Two broad classes of estoppel within which other types of estoppel exist include: 1) **equitable estoppel**, and 2) **collateral estoppel**.

Excess of Loss Reinsurance

The reinsurer agrees to indemnify the primary insurer for all losses exceeding a specified retention either on a per loss basis or an aggregate loss basis.

- *Catastrophe reinsurance contracts* indemnify the ceding company for all losses in excess of a specified amount resulting from a single catastrophic event.

- **Per risk reinsurance contracts** apply to individual risks (most likely part of a facultative agreement) whereby the reinsurer agrees to assume losses over a pre-determined amount. The primary insurer pays all losses up to that point.

- **Per occurrence reinsurance** are similar to catastrophe reinsurance.

- **Aggregate excess of loss** reinsurance agreements stipulate that the reinsurer will pay all primary insurer losses that exceed a specified retention during the contract period. For example, the primary insurer contracts with the reinsurer to insure aggregate losses exceeding $500 million in the period. The primary insurer is indemnified for all loss payments above that amount (subject to the policy limit).

Exculpatory

An agreement altering tort and contract law. The root term exculpate means to hold another blameless for their future actions. Commonly used in waivers to protect one party against injury suits from another party while participating in activities that may prove inherently dangerous. Exculpatory agreements generally cannot be used to avoid statutory requirements, common law duties, criminal penalties or negligence in tort (duties owed to the public cannot be contracted away). If there is unequal bargaining strength between the parties to the contract, an exculpatory clause may be considered unconscionable and thus unenforceable. These rules vary by jurisdiction.

Express Contract

An express contract is one that has been reduced to writing. However, some oral contracts may be given the weight of express contracts provided all requirements of a contract are present (offer, acceptance, consideration, etc.). (See **Implied Contract**)

Extra Expense

Necessary additional expenses that would not have been incurred had no direct property damage occurred.

Fellow Servant Rule

Defense against employer negligence asserting that an employee's injury was caused by a fellow employee not by the acts of the employer.

First Named Insured

Special rights and responsibilities are granted to the first named insured. The first named insured is the only insured with rights to make changes to the policy. Further, this insured is empowered to make the decisions for and speak for all other scheduled insureds. This insured is also responsible for paying the premium and cooperating with the insurance carrier in all matters. Other rights and responsibilities include: the right to cancel the policy, only insured to receive the cancellation notice, and receives any return premium due.

Care must be taken to confirm that the first named insured is the one that the client wants to have all these rights and responsibilities and that this insured is functionally able to manage the relationship.

Flammable Liquids

Liquids having a closed cup flashpoint below 100 degrees Fahrenheit and a vapor pressure not exceeding 40 pounds per square inch. These are known as Class 1 liquids.

- *Class 1A liquids* – flash points below 73 degrees Fahrenheit and boiling points below 100 degrees Fahrenheit
- *Class 1B liquids* – flash points below 73 degrees Fahrenheit and boiling points at or above 100 degrees Fahrenheit
- *Class 1C liquids* – flash points at or above 73 degrees Fahrenheit and below 100 degrees Fahrenheit

Force Majeure

A French phrase that translates to "great or superior force." Force majeure excuses a party from liability for the failure to comply with the provisions of the contract due directly to events beyond the control of that party (i.e. natural disasters, war or uncontrollable failure of a third party to meet its obligations). The potentially liable party is only excused if the event causing non-compliance could not have been foreseen or avoided by the exercise of due diligence in planning and execution.

Foreign Carrier

A carrier operating in a state in which it is not domiciled.

Fraud

A false statement or act intentionally committed by one to gain advantage over or induce another to a particular action to the detriment of the second (the defrauded individual). This is a catch-all category commonly tied in with **concealment** and **misrepresentation**. The main distinction with fraud is that it is an outright intentional act by the defrauding party. Fraud of a material nature will void coverage and may also be a criminal act.

Functional Replacement Cost

Property is valued at the cost necessary to replace damaged or destroyed property with new property of unlike kind and quality. The property performs the same general function allowing the insured to accomplish their business objectives.

Gap Factor

An increase in limit over the amount of the developed business income exposure to account for any unexpected increase in revenue and/or to provide a cushion against any unexpected extension in the period of restoration.

General Contractor

An individual or entity with whom the principal/owner directly contracts to perform specified jobs. Some or all of the enumerated tasks are subsequently contracted to other entities (subcontractors) for performance. Three parties are required before any entity is considered a general contractor: a principal, an independent contractor and a subcontractor hired by the independent contractor. The independent contractor's status changes to that of a general contractor when any part of the work is subcontracted to another entity.

General Exclusions Classifications

These are the opposite of **standard exception** classifications. General exclusion class activities are completely unexpected and are not considered part of the analogy of the governing classification of most operations. Employees engaged in general exclusion activities require separation to allow the insurer to garner the usually higher premium for the increase exposure. Operations and activities falling within the general exclusion classification are: 1) employees working in aircraft operations, 2) employees performing new construction or alterations, 3) stevedoring employees, 4) sawmill operation employees, and 5) employees working in an employer-owned daycare.

General Inclusion Classifications

Some activities are considered to be an integral part of the business' operations thus the payroll of the individuals engaged in these activities is included in the governing classification. These activities include: 1) employees that work in a restaurant, cafeteria or commissary run by the business for use by the employees (this does not apply to such establishments at construction sites), 2) employees manufacturing containers such as boxes, bags, can or cartons for the employer's use in shipping its own products, 3) staff working in hospitals or medical facilities operated by the employer for use by the employees, 4) Maintenance or repair shop employees, and 5) printing or lithography employees engaged in printing for the employer's own products.

Ghost Policy

A ghost policy is a workers' compensation policy written for an unincorporated business with no employees and which does not extend coverage to the business' owner(s). Also applies to an incorporated business with no employees other than the corporate officers who have chosen to exclude themselves from protection.

Hazard

A circumstance which increases the probability of a loss; a source of danger. A hazard increases the frequency and/or severity of a loss. There are four types of hazards with which insureds and insurers must concern themselves.

- **Physical Hazard** – Result from the physical characteristics of the surroundings, equipment or machinery. Such hazards include slippery floors, improper storage of flammable or combustible liquids, frayed wires or worn tires.

- **Moral Hazard** – A subjective measure of the character and circumstances of an insured. Loss arises out of the dishonest actions of a person or group intent on profiting in some way from the injury or damage.

- **Morale Hazard** – A subjective measure of the insured's attitude towards safety and protection. Loss often arises out of carelessness, inattention or indifference.

- **Legal Hazard** – Potential increase in the cost of a loss resulting from court actions. An example would be a punitive damages award.

Immediately Dangerous to Life and Health (IDLH)

A standard of measure collaboratively developed by the National Institute for Occupational Safety and Health (NIOSH) and the Occupational Safety and Health Administration (OSHA). Three hundred eight-seven (387) chemicals known or suspected to cause death or severe injuries when in sufficient concentration were studied to aid in respirator development and selection. Permissible exposure levels (chemical concentrations) were assigned below which an otherwise healthy employee could be exposed, without the aid of a respirator, for up to 30 minutes without: 1) immediate or delayed loss or life, 2) experiencing any long-term, irreversible health effects, or even 3) suffering severe eye or respiratory tract infection or any other debilitating problem that could prevent escape from the area.

NIOSH and OSHA warned in their initial publication that the "30-minute" standard allowed for a margin of error and was not meant to imply that it was safe for an employee to remain in the environment in the absence of an appropriate respirator any longer than it took to escape. Original permissible exposure levels were based on limited toxicological data. In the mid-1990's permissible exposure concentrations were lowered across the board and 80 known or potential carcinogens were added and detailed.

Implied Contract

Implied contracts are oral or understood agreements or promises between parties generally created by actions or the assumed intentions of the parties or the surrounding circumstances.

Including

Including within this definition of **occurrence** is not simply a consequence of repeated or prolonged exposure to a condition. For there to be a true **occurrence**, there must first be an accident causing injury or damage. A sudden and unexpected incident must take place leading to prolonged exposure resulting in injury or damage for there to be a true

occurrence. It's a question of cause and effect, there must be an unbroken chain of events beginning with an initial incident before prolonged exposure is considered an occurrence as including.

Indemnitor

The party called on to respond financially. This can include the **Transferee** or an insurance company.

Independent Contractor

An entity with whom a principal/owner directly contracts to perform a task or tasks. Independent contractors are generally engaged to perform operations not within the usual trade or business of the principal and such tasks are contract-specific. All work required of the contract is performed by the independent contractor and employees.

Insurable Business Income

The amount of business income used to calculate the business income premium – the "J.1." total. This amount includes all of an entity's operating expenses with the exception of a few non-continuing sales-related and production-related expenses to arrive at the insurable business income amount. Whether these other expenses continue, are reduced or disappear during the period of restoration doesn't matter.

Interchange of Labor Rule

The interchange of labor rule is an exception to the governing classification rule. Applicability of this rule varies by state. Some states only allow its use in the construction, erection or stevedoring classes of business while other states permit the interchange of labor rule to apply to any type of business operation. Interchange of labor rules allow a single employee's payroll to be split between or among several class codes that may be present within the operations. Certain requirements must be met before this rule can be applied.

Intermediate Transfer

The **transferee** agrees to accept the financial consequences of **occurrences** caused in whole or in part by its negligence. This includes if the **transferor** or another entity contributes to the loss in some way.

Intestacy

An individual, owning property in excess of debts and expenses (a positive net worth), who dies without a legally binding will or declaration. English law of intestacy under feudalism stated that real property of individuals dying without a legally binding will passed to heirs and personal property passed to the state or the church. As feudalism disappeared, the English adopted Roman law regarding intestacy, similar to the law now applied in America. Common law in America allows all property, real and personal, to pass to provable heirs of intestate individuals (the law of descent).

Some state statutes limit the degrees of separation for an individual to quality as an heir (i.e. "... no more than five degrees from one decedent, not including the decedent..." as specified in one state law). Under current law, if no heir of the intestate individual meeting the requirements can be found, the property (real property and chattel) escheats to the "crown" (the state). Laws govern how the property will be used by the state and which agency is responsible for its distribution.

Inverse Condemnation

A governmental action that diminishes or in practicality removes all value of an individual's property without just compensation. Such action amounts to the regulatory taking of property without actually condemning it and paying the owner its fair market value. The last line of the Fifth Amendment reads as follows: "...nor shall private property be taken for public use, without just compensation."

Such actions generally assume the form of a denial of a permit or the blocking of an individual property owner's ability to use his property in a manner consistent with local zoning use laws, or by enforcing eminent domain in the taking of some property but not all, thus rendering the remaining property useless. Government violating an individual's right to quiet enjoyment of his property by building an airport next to his house is an example (the ultimate effect being the nearly complete devaluation of the property), or other such over-regulation rendering the property valueless. Inverse condemnation is excluded in most public official's liability (POL) policies.

"In the course..."

A function of the timing and location of the injury or illness. The implication is that the injury must occur during operations for the employer, or during employment, and at the employer's location or a location mandated or reasonably expected by the employer.

Jurisdictional Authority Rule

States using this as the measure of **major damage** allow the authority having jurisdiction (the local government) to decide when a damaged building just be brought into compliance with the current building code.

Last Clear Chance

A doctrine in tort law applicable in jurisdictions that subscribe to the contributory negligence doctrine. Last clear chance allows a plaintiff that is contributorily negligent to recover if he is able to prove that the defendant (most at-fault party) had the last opportunity to avoid the accident. Essentially, the plaintiff's negligence is no longer part of the equation. The defendant had time and ability to prevent the accident and failed to take necessary action.

Restated in Legalese: A showing, by the plaintiff, of something new and sequential which affords the defendant a fresh opportunity (of which the defendant fails to avail himself or herself) to avert the consequence of his original negligence.

There are four applicable categories of Last Clear Chance applied by the five remaining jurisdictions that utilize the contributory negligence rule.

- **Helpless Plaintiff** – The plaintiff's initial negligence put him in a position from which he was powerless to escape by ordinary means. The defendant detects the danger with ample time to respond, but fails to act as a reasonable person would.
- **Inattentive Plaintiff** – The plaintiff did not pay attention to his surroundings putting himself in danger. The defendant discovers the peril and has time to respond, but fails to respond to avoid the accident.
- **Observant Defendant** – The defendant actually sees the plaintiff in time to react and safely avoid the incident but negligently fails to respond as a reasonable person would.
- **Inattentive Defendant** – The defendant simply fails to pay attention as a reasonable person should (cell phone use is a good example) and is unable to respond to the plaintiff's helpless condition in time to avoid the accident.

Law of Large Numbers

A foundational insurance concept stating that the greater the number of homogenous (alike) exposures there are, the closer actual results come to matching predicted outcomes. In insurance terms: the more houses (cars, restaurants, etc.) an insurance carrier insures, the more accurately they will be able to predict losses.

The classic example used to explain the law of large numbers is a coin flip. There are two options, heads or tails, each having a 50/50 chance of occurring on each toss. The more times the coin is flipped, the closer the results will be to a 50/50 frequency. If the coin is flipped only 10 times, the result may be seven heads and three tails. If the coin is flipped 1,000 times the frequency could change to 60% heads and 40% tails. The more flips, the closer the frequency of heads and tails will come to a 50/50 split (the predicted outcome).

Leader Location

These can include anchor stores, sports and entertainment venues and other such operations or entities that draw customers to the area or drive them to the insured location. (aka drivers)

Legal Person (aka Juridical Person)

A legal fiction, a "person" created by statute and "born" with the filing of articles of incorporation (or organization). These legal persons are given the right to own property, sue and be sued. Corporations are legal persons. Several states consider LLC's a legal person making the managers and members employees.

Libel/Slander

False statements broadcast about a person as fact not opinion. These statements do not have to be made with the intent to harm or shame to allow for a tort claim, but if done with malice, the injured party can sue for general damages in addition to special damages. Libelous statements are generally written or broadcast through the media (television, radio and the Internet) while slander deals with the spoken word (it doesn't linger and is generally directed to a known audience). Both terms can be classified as defamation.

Defamation can be defended in several ways.

- **Truth** – Truth is an absolute defense. If the information broadcast is true, the "injured" party does not have a right to sue provided the information was not personal and not a matter of public concern (such as releasing a private citizen's medical records).
- **Privilege** – Statements made in court or other like venues are generally exempt from defamation.
- **Opinion** – This defense is not allowed in all jurisdictions, but if the statement was the broadcaster's opinion, he has not defamed the individual. Context

and relationship are considered when opinion is used as a defense.

- **Unintentional ("innocent") dissemination** – When the individual passed along information he/she thought was true but wasn't (this is usually called gossip).
- **Public Figure** – People in the eye of the public have less personal rights to privacy (even if they did not put themselves in the public eye purposefully). To bring a successfully libel or slander suit, they must prove actual malice and harm.

Limited Common Elements (Condominiums)

Limited common elements benefits more than one but less than all unit owners. Common hallways or corridors providing access to several units, walls and columns containing electrical wiring or sprinkler piping serving or protecting multiple units or a plenum enclosure providing heating and cooling to multiple units are examples. Doorsteps, stoops, decks, porches, balconies, patios, exterior doors and windows or other fixtures designed to serve a single unit but located outside the unit's boundaries are often categorized as limited common elements because the appearance and safety of these fixtures directly affect multiple unit owners although connected to just one unit.

Limited Liability Corporation (LLC)

An LLC is a hybrid legal entity combining the advantages (mostly tax based) of a partnership and the liability protection offered by a corporation. Members are simply the owners of the LLC and may or may not participate in the day-to-day management of the company. Members involved in the management maintain a dual role as a member and a manager.

Limited Transfer

The narrowest level of contractual risk transfer. The **transferee** only accepts the financial consequences of loss resulting from his/its sole negligence. If the **transferor** or another party contributes to the loss, the **transferee** is not financially responsible for that part of the loss. Essentially, the **transferor** is only protected for its vicarious liability arising out of the actions of the **transferee**.

Liquidated Damages

A contractual agreement requiring one party to pay another a specified amount of certain contractual provisions are violated or are not completed. Liquidated damages are necessary when actual damages are difficult to calculate or estimate at the beginning of the contract.

Major Damage

The amount of damage required for the jurisdictional authority to require the structure be brought into compliance with the current building code. See **Jurisdictional Authority Rule** and **Percentage Rule**.

Majority Interest (Combinability)

Majority interest is created when the same person or group of person(s) combine to own more than 50% of an entity and can be created in many ways: 1) An entity or persons (as detailed above) owns the majority of the voting stock of another entity, or both entities share a majority of the same owners (if there is no voting stock). Generally these are natural persons that own multiple entities. 2) If neither of the above applies, majority interest is created if a majority of the board is common between two or among several entities. 3) Participation of each general partner in the profits of the partnership (limited partners are excluded). 4) When ownership interest is held by an entity as a fiduciary (excludes a debtor in possession, a trustee under an irrevocable trust or a franchisor).

Manufacturing Location

A dependent property location that manufactures "products for delivery to your customers under contract for sale." (aka "Provider")

Market Value

Negotiated between and agreed to by a willing buyer and a willing seller. It can fluctuate up and down based on the economy, condition, use or need and has little relation to the true cost to rebuild a particular structure. Normally market value has little relationship to insurance.

Material Fact

Information or data supplied by the insured, the truth and accuracy of which the insurer relies on to make an underwriting decision. Three tests are applied when deciding if a fact is material or merely informational. A fact is material if the underwriter would have made a different underwriting decision, charged a different premium, or applied different terms and conditions.

Maximum Coinsurance Percentage

Number of months required to accomplish the four period of restoration objectives / 12 (the number of months in a year)

Maximum Possible Loss

Maximum possible loss is the worst case scenario and the most pessimistic view – the entire building and everything inside could be destroyed (such loss could be considered a shock loss). Other terms for maximum possible loss are amount subject to loss and maximum foreseeable loss.

Maximum Probable Loss

Maximum probable loss is inversely proportional to the size of a structure and the effectiveness of any protective safeguards. The larger the building, the less likely the entire property will be destroyed; and the better the fire protection (sprinklers, alarms and public protection) the more likely a fire will be contained and extinguished before the entire building is destroyed. The occupancy and contents within the building also affect the amount of damage likely to occur. Probably maximum loss (PML) is alternative terminology.

Misrepresentation

A dressed-up term for an overt lie. This is a knowingly false statement made in the application and depended on by the underwriter to arrive at an underwriting decision. However, this term is not equivalent to a warranty. The root of this term is "representation" meaning that the information is true to be the best of the insured's knowledge. The information is not guaranteed, thus it is not a warranty of accuracy (which implies absolute truth). "To the best of the insured's knowledge" gives room for unintentional misrepresentation where a guarantee or warranty does not.

Mold Triangle

There are three elements necessary for formation and growth of mold.

- *Food source* – Mold thrives on cellulose in building related products, paper, dust and food. Many other organic materials can be food for mold.
- *Optimal temperatures* – Mold tends to thrive best in temperatures between 60 degrees and 80 degrees Fahrenheit.

- ***Water*** – The last side of the triangle is a steady supply of water. Water can come from leakage and infiltration or high humidity. This is critical to mold growth; take away the water and mold will not grow.

Monopolistic States

Employers can purchase a workers' compensation policy only for the state. Only four monopolistic states are still in operation: North Dakota, Ohio, Washington and Wyoming. Employers' liability coverage is not offered by these states and this coverage must be procured by alternative means.

Natural Person

A flesh and blood human being. In workers' compensation the employer is a natural person(s) in sole proprietorships and partnerships. Managers and members of an LLC are viewed as natural persons in a majority of states making these natural persons the employers.

Non-Delegable Duty

A requirement placed on one individual or entity by reason of relationship which cannot be passed to a third party. For instance, an employer is responsible for keeping the workplace safe, training employees and assuring safety for its customers (within their control); these requirements cannot be transferred by contract.

Non-Special Flood Hazard Area (non-SFHA's)

Non-special flood hazard areas are historically delineated with "B," "C" or X." These are considered areas of moderate or minimal flooding hazard, generally only expected to flood in times of severe storms and weather conditions or when drainage problems exist. However, 25% to 30% of all flood insurance claims are paid in these "less hazardous" areas.

Zones historically labeled "B" and "C" are being replaced with "X." As Flood Insurance Rate Maps are updated, non-SFHA's will be assigned a "Shaded X" or an un-shaded "X." Base flood elevations are not indicated in either "X" zone.

"Shaded X" zones correspond to areas with a higher probability of flooding than areas tagged by an un-shaded "X." A "Shaded X" indicates the area has a 0.2% annual chance of flooding (the "500-year" flood line) or a 1% chance of experiencing flooding of less than one foot in any given year (not high enough to be classified as a special flood hazard area).

Areas where the flood hazard is undetermined are labeled on the FIRMs with a zone "D." This zone may also be used when one community incorporates portions of another community where no map has been previously prepared.

Occupational Disease

Illness directly attributable to work conditions and exposures; such injury or illness must arise out of and in the course and scope of employment. To be considered occupational and therefore compensable, the disease must arise out of or be caused by conditions peculiar to the work. Medical opinion leading to the conclusion that an illness is work-related is not necessarily based on the disease but on the facts surrounding the patient's sickness.

Occurrence

An **accident**, including continuous or repeated exposure to substantially the same general harmful conditions.

Operational Capability

An entity's ability to operate at or near pre-loss production or sales capacity. This is a non-policy business income term describing the point at which a manufacturing operation can return to pre-loss production levels and inventory levels (excluding the recreation of finished stock) and a non-manufacturing entity can operate with the same level of inventory, equipment and efficiency as before the operation closing loss.

Operational Continuity

The ability of the business to continue to operate and produce some amount of goods or services following a loss-induced business suspension.

Ordinary Employee

These are employees not classified as officers, executives, department managers, employees under contract or any specifically listed employee or job description.

Ordinary Payroll

Payroll of **ordinary employees**

Original Specifications

Term used in relation to condominiums. Like **all in**, the association is responsible for insuring **common elements**, **limited common elements** and unit real property. However, any improvements made by the unit owners are not the responsibility of the association but the unit owner.

A majority of statutes default to some form of original specification wording as recommended by the Uniform Common Interest Ownership Act to govern the insurance requirements of condominium associations.

Participating Community

An NFIP participating community is one that: 1) has been notified by FEMA through the Federal Insurance and Mitigation Administration (FIMA) that there are flood-prone areas within the community (usually resulting from previous floods), 2) have been notified of the location of those areas by publication of a Flood Hazard Boundary Map, 3) within one year of notifications agrees to join NFIP, and 4) agrees to participate in the development of local flood plain management guidelines. Being labeled a participating community is the first step toward becoming a regular community.

Percentage Rule

States and jurisdictions applying this rule require a building damaged beyond a certain percentage of its value be brought, in its entirety, into compliance with local building code.

Period of Restoration

The period of time that begins after the direct physical loss or damage by a Covered Cause of Loss at the described premises. A time deductible applies and differs based on the coverage (BI or EE) and ends on the earlier of: 1) the date when the property at the described premises should be repaired, rebuilt or replaced with reasonable speed and similar quality, or 2) the date when the business is resumed at a new permanent location.

Permanent Partial Disability

The employee has suffered an injury from which he will never recover, but one that will not prevent him from returning to some type of work. Amputation of a finger or leg, the loss of an eye or ear are examples of this injury classification.

Permanent Total Disability

Recovery is not predicted. The employee is not expected to ever be able to return to work. Full paralysis, total blindness and total loss of hearing are examples of such an injury.

Personal Injury

Usually describes intentional torts such as libel, slander, defamation of character, false arrest, wrongful entry into, wrongful eviction from, malicious prosecution and other such actions.

Post-FIRM

Structures completed or substantially improved after the issuance of the community's initial flood insurance rate map (FIRM).

Pre-Construction Duties

Development and approval of the new building plans; advertising for, interviewing and selecting a general contractor; applying for and waiting on building permits; and scheduling and completing site clearance work.

Pre-FIRM

Structures completed or substantially improved prior to the issuance of the community's initial flood insurance rate map (FIRM).

Pre-Loss Operational Income

The ability to generate revenues at the same level enjoyed prior to the suspension of operations.

Products Liability

Related to **strict liability**. Defective product design or manufacture which results in an injury makes the manufacturer strictly liability. The injured party need not prove negligence in the design or manufacture, only that the product's design or method of manufacture was defective, making it unreasonably dangerous and the ultimate cause of injury.

Production-Related Expenses

Cost of goods sold (COGS); Outside services resold; Utility services which do not continue under contract; Ordinary payroll; and Special deductions for mining operations

Pro-Rata Reinsurance

The primary insurer cedes a predetermined percentage of the risk to the reinsurer. The reinsurer shares in the losses proportional to the premiums and limits reinsured. Two major types of pro rata reinsurance are quota share and surplus share.

- **Quota share agreements** require the primary insurer to cede a certain percentage of every risk within the agreement to the reinsurer (paying a proportional premium). In return, the reinsurer agrees to indemnify losses suffered by the ceding company in the same proportion. If the reinsurer agrees to reinsure 35% of the risk (accepting a proportional premium for that agreement, they pay 35% of any losses.

- **Surplus share agreements** allow the primary insurer to cede a certain percentage of liabilities exceeding a pre-determined retention. The ceded amount can vary from risk to risk. Premiums and losses are received and paid by the reinsurer in the same proportion.

Punitive Damages

Meant to punish the wrongdoer whose actions are egregious, willful, wanton or malicious. The amount is intended to warn others to avoid such actions.

Pure Risk

There are only two possibilities; something bad happening or nothing happening. It is unlikely that any measurable benefit will arise from a pure risk. The house will enjoy a year with nothing bad occurring or there will be damage caused by a covered case of loss (fire, wind, etc.). Predicting the outcomes of a pure risk is accomplished (sometimes) using the **law of large numbers**, **a priori data** or **empirical data**. Pure risk, also known as absolute risk, is insurable.

Putative Employer

The special employer rather than the direct employer. Status as the employer of record at such a specific time is "put" upon the individual or entity based on several factors, the most obvious is the amount of control the person/entity has over the worker.

Qui Tam

Allowed by the Federal Civil False Claims Act (31 U.S.C. Section 3729 et seq), a qui tam is a suit brought by a private citizen in the name of and on behalf of the United States. Such suits are usually based on charges of fraud committed by government contractors or others who use or receive governmental funds. The individual that brings suit can share in any of the monies recovered. The intent of this law was to allow citizens to benefit from acting on the government's behalf when the citizen spots fraud the government may not see. Citizens (whistleblowers) that bring a qualified qui tam suit can receive between 15% and 30% of the returned money; according to several reports, over $2 billion has been recovered (over $350 million has gone to the whistleblowers).

Recipient Location

A dependent property location that buys/accepts the products, goods or services of the insured. (aka "Buyer")

Reinsurance

Insurance for insurance companies. Primary insurance carriers "cede" some portion of the risks they agree to underwrite (based on the design of the reinsurance contract) to a reinsurance carrier (known as the cedant). Primary insurers and reinsurers negotiate and re-negotiate these contracts based on market conditions, trends and loss history.

Reinsurance contracts often influence (limit) the risks primary insurance carriers underwrite. An insurer's capacity and appetite is proportional to the availability and use of reinsurance: the lower the reinsurer's capacity, the lower the primary insurer's capacity; and the narrower the reinsurer's appetite, the narrower the appetite of the primary insurer.

Reinsurers can also reinsure their exposure through retrocession, reinsurance for the reinsurer.

Reinsurance is vital to the insurance mechanism, especially in light of the global insurance economy. Reinsurance accomplishes four functions/goals.

1. Stabilizes the earnings of the primary insurer (in the event of catastrophic losses).
2. Increases primary insurer capacity by limiting liability on individual risks.
3. Provides liquidity, protecting against swings in business cycles.

4. Provides underwriting expertise to the primary insurer.

Replacement Cost

The cost to replace with new material of like kind and quality on the date of the loss. There is no allowance or penalty for age, depreciation or condition.

Respondeat Superior

Latin for let the master answer.

Risk Control

Risk control is establishing a plane to reduce the possibility of a loss occurring, or to lessen the effect if one does occur. One or a combination of the following is used in risk control.

- *Loss control* – constitutes: 1) prevention of losses by design or planning to keep the loss from occurring; and 2) reduction of losses by design or planning to lessen the effect of a loss if one does occur.
- *Avoidance* – deciding not to undertake the activity to avoid any chance of incurring a loss.
- *Transfer* – the activity to another party, thus removing the liability for any loss that does occur by placing it on the other party.

Risk Financing

Risk financing is developing and planning for a source of financing necessary to cover the consequences of any loss. Use of one or more of the following financing techniques is common.

- *Insurance* – the most common means of financing a loss.
- *Retention* – the entity chooses to pay all potential losses out of available cash. This is rarely a viable option for most individuals or businesses.
- *Transfer* – usually accomplished by contract where one entity (not an insurance company) agrees to bear the financial consequences of a loss suffered by the business.

Risk Management in its broadest sense is divided into two main categories: **risk financing** and **risk control.**

Rolling Total

Relates to pure extra expense coverage provided in the CP 00 50 (Extra Expense Coverage Form). The insured chooses a rolling total payout percentage, meaning that the insured has access to progressively higher percentages of the total limit during each 30 day period.

Sales Related Expenses

- Pre-paid outgoing freight, returns and allowances and discounts as costs associated with the post-production sales process.

- Bad debt that cannot be collected from buyers of the insured's product.
- Collection expenses that reduce the amount of cash available to cover business-related expenses and generate a profit.

"Scope of employment..."

Analyzes the motivations of the employee, the employer's discretion and control over the actions of the employee and the employer's foresee ability of the activities of the employee. Employee actions which ultimately lead to an accident or injury must be motivated, in whole or in part, by the desire to further the interests of the employer. Motivation or desire can be out of fear that failure to perform will result in the loss of a job, or from a more altruistic desire to do well for the employer. The basis for the motivation or desire is irrelevant; it is the fact that the motivation exists that leads to compensability. Further, the actions must, to some extent, be at the presumed direction of the employer or potentially foreseen by the employer.

Shear Walls

A shear wall is a structural support running parallel (as nearly as possible) to the flow of water. These walls are not structurally joined at the ends allowing rushing water to flow through unimpeded.

Significant Contact Test

This test is applied when making jurisdictional decisions – which state benefits can the employee access. Significant contact tests base these jurisdictional decisions around the employee. Three primary tests/questions work to determine which states need to be scheduled as primary, 3.A. states. These questions are: 1) Where does the employee live? 2) Where does the employee primarily work? And 3) In what state was the contract of hire made? If a preponderance of contact evidences a state not listed as a 3.A. state, there may be a gap in protection.

Situs

The first test before an employee can be considered a longshoreman or harbor worker. Situs requires that the employment be on, above, or below navigable waters and adjoining areas. However, working around or over water does not in itself qualify an individual for the benefits prescribed by USL&HW Act law. To qualify for such coverage requires satisfying the status test.

SLAPP

A Strategic Lawsuit Against Public Participation (SLAPP) is an assault using the legal system as the weapon of choice.

Individuals, corporations and governments file SLAPP suits packaged to look like civil suits alleging defamation, invasion of privacy, nuisance, malicious prosecution and other personal injury charges intended solely to embezzle the "offender's" time and finances by means of legal wrangling and continually mounting legal costs. Most individuals and small businesses do not have the time or the financial resources to invest in their defense choosing rather to end the publication or protest. Not only does this remove the primary thorn from the plaintiff's side, but this tactic produces sufficient fear to keep others from voicing their beliefs.

Anti-SLAPP statutes make such suits illegal. Twenty-seven states* currently have anti-SLAPP statutes on the books. Defendants in these states providing a SLAPP suit generally prevail in court, provided all other standards of journalist responsibility have been satiated.
(*These states are: AR, CA, CO, DE, FL, GA, HI, IN, LA, ME, MD, MA, MN, MO, NE, NV, NM, NY, OK, OR, PA, RI, TN, UT, WA, WV, and WI)

Special Flood Hazard Areas (SFHA's)

A special flood hazard area is a specifically defined area that has a 1% chance of being inundated by flood waters in any given year (thus the creation of the term "100-year flood plain"). Flood waters have an equal chance of submerging these areas every year for five straight years, or not for 200 years; there is simply a 1% statistical possibility every year. Homes located in special flood hazard areas have a 26% chance of suffering flood damage over the normal 30-year life of a loan according to FEMA.

There are two broad classifications of special flood hazard areas: 1) "A" zones, and 2) "V" zones. Detailed information about these zones is often found on Flood Insurance Rate Maps (FIRM's) using sub-classifications such as "AR," "AO" or "VO." These and other SFHA sub-classifications provide information about the pattern and characteristics of flooding in the specified area. Information about each of the Special Flood Hazard Area sub-classifications can be found online.

Speculative Risk

Three possible outcomes exist in speculative risk: something good (gain), something bad (loss) or nothing (staying even). Gambling and investing in the stock market are two examples of speculative risks. Each offers a chance to make money, lose money or walk away even. Again, do not equate gambling and investing on any other level than as both being a speculative risk. Gambling is designed to enrich one party (the house), the odds are always in its favor. Investing is designed to enrich al involved, the house that set up the "game" and those that chose to place money in the game. All participants with "skin in the game" win or lose together. Speculative risk is not insurable in the traditional insurance market. There are other means to hedge speculative risk such as diversification and derivatives.

Standard Exception Classifications

Some duties/activities are considered so common to most business and/or such duties may be so far outside the operational activities of the business that employees engaged in these activities are considered exceptions to the governing classification rules. Payroll for these standard exception classes of employees is subtracted from the governing classification and assigned to the applicable standard exception code and rated separately from the governing class. The standard exception classes include: 1) Clerical Employees – Class Code 8810; 2) Clerical Telecommuter – Class Code 8871; 3) Drafting Employees – Class Code 8810; 4) Salespersons – Class Code 8742; and 5) Drivers – Class Code 7380.

Standard exception classifications are not necessarily limited to these five class codes. Some states utilize state-specific class codes that are also eligible for assignment as a standard exception.

Status

To be considered a longshoreman or harbor worker requires that the employment involve the loading and unloading of ships; or the maintenance or dismantling of ships.

Strict Liability

Absolute liability (another term for strict liability) is imposed on the party who causes harm, regardless of intent or the need to prove negligence. Simply the fact that injury or damage occurred make the party liable. Strict liability's reach is essentially limited to: **products liability; ultra**

hazardous operations; care and keeping of animals (especially those with a propensity towards viciousness, making the owner strictly liable for any injury the animal causes); and **strict liability by statute.**

Strict liability is supported by the philosophy that the benefits derived from holding the individual or entity responsible for the damage, regardless of intent or negligence, are greater than the burden placed on the liable party. Improved product safety and design result from the application of strict liability.

Strict Liability by Statute

Some jurisdictions modify laws such that specific actions resulting in injury automatically make the offending party liable just because of the action.

Subrogation

Individuals or entities suffering injury and/or damage due to the negligence of another person or entity have the right to recover costs and expenses from the at-fault party. If, however, the injured party chooses to seek reimbursement from its own insurance carrier, the rights of the injured party are transferred to the insurance carrier. Subrogation rights for the insurance carrier flow from the right of its insured to recover payment. If the insured does not have the right to recover payment, neither does its insurance carrier. Contractual risk transfer provisions often limit the rights of one party to recover from another party for injury or damage. When the right of the insured to recover is waived via a contract, the insurer's right to subrogate is lost.

Takaful

An Islamic insurance concept based on Islamic law (Sharia). The Takaful system is based on mutual cooperation and assurance between and among the group or individuals protected. In some sense it's like a true, classic mutual insurance company (best comparison available) or cooperative insurance. The foundational goal is to "bear ye one another's burdens" without the goal of earning a profit. Money is pooled and paid out as needed. Traditional insurance is against Muslim belief as, according to their beliefs, it involves uncertainty, gambling and interest. Various levels and application of this concept exist.

Temporary Partial Disability

An injury from which the employee is expected to completely recover in some period of time with little or no long-term effects. A broken arm is a good example if this type of injury. Employees suffering temporary partial injuries can generally return to work under light-duty assignments until the temporary condition heals.

Temporary Total Disability

A full recovery from the injury is expected, but for a period of time the employee is completely unable to work due to the injury. These types of injuries might require bed rest or hospitalization while the employee recovers.

Time Doctrine

All business income losses are settled based on the coverage limit purchased. An accurate business income coverage limit calculation depends on the legitimate estimation of the worst-case **period of restoration**. Estimating the worst-case **period of restoration** necessitates understanding the time required to accomplish each of the 10 steps in the four **period of restoration** objectives. The key to business income is the correct estimation of time.

Transferee

The party accepting the risk in a contractual risk transfer agreement. This can include the general contractor and subcontractors. Other common terms include the indemnitor and promisor.

Transferor

The party from whom risk is being transferred in a contractual risk transfer agreement. This may include the owner, the project management firm, and/or the general contractor. Other common terms for the transferor include indemnitee and promisee.

Trespass for Deceit

Could also be titled "Trespass by Deceit." Courts of fifteenth century England likened injury caused by failure to live up to a contract to injury caused by tort as both assign risks and duties owed. A tradesman that contracted to perform a certain task and did it poorly was equated to a trespasser that entered the property and caused damage. As contract law matured, relating breaches of contract to tort law gradually disappeared, but the term still appears in contract case law on occasion.

Ultra-Hazardous Operations

Related to **strict liability**. Also known as an inherently dangerous activity. Within the rule of strict or absolute liability, an ultra-hazardous operation is where the owner of the land conducts or allows the conduct of an activity or operation which is dangerous to the neighbors in the immediate area by the activity's very nature. The Second Restatement of Torts rule 520 applies six tests to judge whether an activity is ultra-hazardous.

1. There is a high degree of risk that some harm will come to person(s), land or chattels of others.
2. There is a high probability that any harm will be severe.
3. The ability or inability to reduce the risk by exercise of reasonable care.
4. How far outside the common usage of the property the activity undertaken is.

5. Is the activity appropriate relative to the place where it is conducted?

6. Do the values and benefits derived from the activity outweigh its dangerous attributes?

Unconscionable

A contract or contract provision that is unreasonable due to the unequal bargaining strength of the parties, or the result of the undue influence or unfair tactics.

Unit Improvements and Betterments

Like unit property benefit none but the unit owner. A unit improvements and betterments is created by the unit owner's engagement in any activity or improvement that increases the value of the real property within an individual unit – such as updating the flooring from carpet to hardwood or other such improvements.

Unit Property

Defined by the association's declarations or statute and is limited to and benefits none but the unit owner. The inside of the exterior walls, interior partition walls, counter tops, cabinetry, plumbing fixtures, appliances and any other real property confined to the unit are examples.

Void

As if it never existed. In essence if certain acts are committed or policy provisions ignored, the insurance policy has no legal effect and is unenforceable on the insurance carrier.

Concealment or **misrepresentation** of a **material fact**, and **fraud** can render an insurance policy void ab initio (that is, from the beginning). Since the policy has never legally existed, there is no coverage provided now or in the future.

Zone of Danger

Could the person have been injured by the negligent actions of another? If so, that person is considered to be within the zone of danger. Most jurisdictions allow bystanders in this zone of danger to sue for negligent infliction of emotional distress even if they are not physically injured. If you are on a street corner waiting to cross the street and a car comes speeding around the corner, hits another car, loses control and skids to a stop just inches from you, you can sue even though you were not actually injured. Some jurisdictions do not require the plaintiff to be in harm's way, but only requires that they witness the injury of a loved one caused by the negligence of another.

Author Biography

Christopher J. Boggs joined the insurance industry in 1990 and is a self-proclaimed insurance geek with a true passion for the insurance profession and a desire for continual learning.

During his career, Boggs has authored hundreds of insurance and risk management-related articles on a wide range of topics as diverse as Credit Default Swaps, the MCS-90, and enterprise risk management.

A graduate of Liberty University with a bachelor's degree in Journalism, Boggs has continually pursued career-related education, obtaining nine professional insurance designations: the Chartered Property Casualty Underwriter (**CPCU**), Associate in Risk Management (**ARM**), Associate in Loss Control Management (**ALCM**), Legal Principles Claims Management (**LPCS**), Accredited Advisor in Insurance (**AAI**), Associate in Premium Auditing (**APA**), Certified Workers' Compensation Advisor (**CWCA**), Construction Risk and Insurance Specialist (**CRIS**) and the Associate in General Insurance (**AINS**) designations.

Made in the USA
Monee, IL
27 April 2024